Palmistry

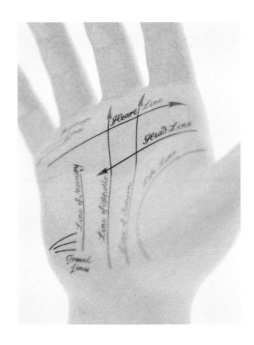

Palmistry

Sasha Fenton

© 2007 D&S Books Ltd
© 2010 Kerswell Farm Ltd

This edition published by King Books

Printed 2012

This book is distributed in the UK by
Parkham Books Ltd
Barns Farm, Boraston
Tenbury Wells
Worcestershire
WR15 8NB

david@kingbooks.co.uk

ISBN: 978-1-906239-39-8

DS0153. Palmistry

Creative Director: Sarah King
Project Editor: Clare Bone
Designer: Debbie Fisher & Co

Printed in Singapore

Material from this book previously appeared in Palmistry - a beginner's guide.

1 3 5 7 9 10 8 6 4 2

CONTENTS

Introduction to palmistry   6

Observing hands   12

The map of the hand   24

The fingers and thumb   30

The mounts   54

The lines of the hand   67

Marks   132

Health on the hands   142

Taking handprints   152

Psychic development   156

Index   158

Acknowledgements   160

Bibliography   160

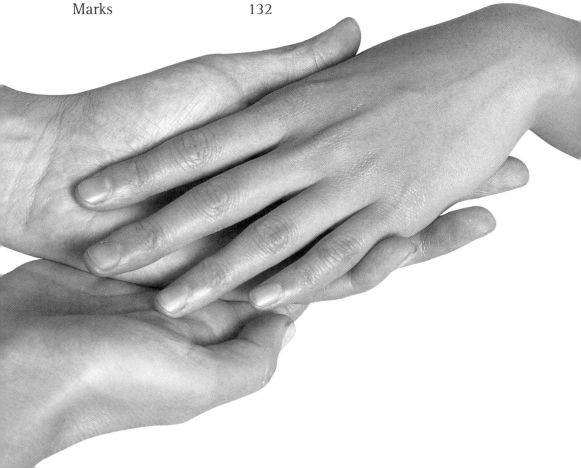

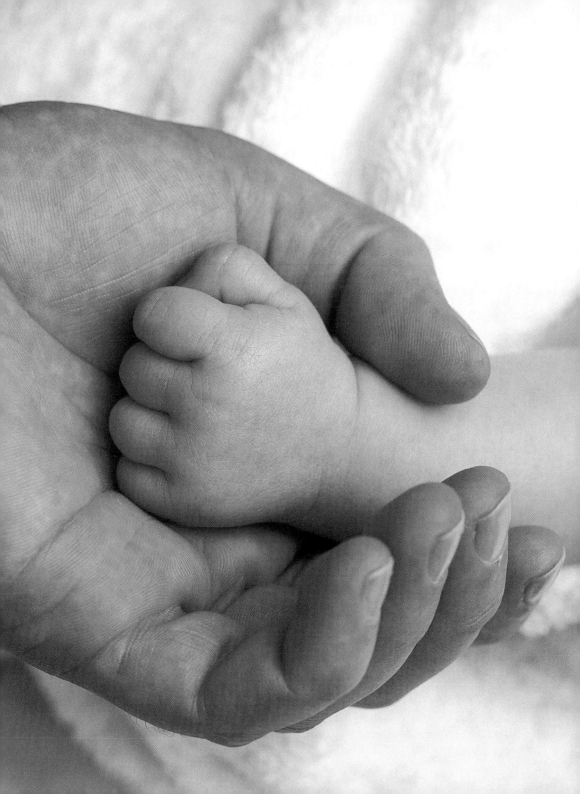

INTRODUCTION TO PALMISTRY

Have you ever watched a really young baby? When an infant takes his first look at the world around him, he starts by studying his hands, peering at them intently as though they were strange objects that he needs to become accustomed to – which, indeed, they are.

When people are extremely upset or in a state of shock, they peer at their hands in exactly the same infantile way, almost as though they were seeing them for the first time. It appears that our hands are our initial link between the external world and our own bodies, and the first part of ourselves that we seek to understand.

Primitive humans made outlines of hands in cave paintings. The early artist would place his, or someone else's, hand on a rock face and then spray a mouthful of coloured soil on to it, which solidified, leaving an outline of the hand. It is fascinating to think that a hand-reader can glean information about

the artist or his subject all these thousands of years later. The same goes for the handprints that famous film stars impress into the cement along Sunset Boulevard in Los Angeles – even those distorted images tell us more about the star than he or she might want us to know.

There is mention of hand-reading in the Bible, notably in the famous passage about the woman of worth, whose length of days is in her right hand and riches in her left. Whoever wrote that passage must have been looking into the hands of a left-handed woman! As far back as 497 BC, Pythagoras wrote about hand-reading, but from those early days to the 19th-century explosion of interest in the subject, the art was mainly confined to the areas that we now know as Pakistan and Afghanistan, where it was practised by the Gypsies. From the 13th century onwards, the expansion of the Turks drove some Gypsy tribes from their lands, after which they migrated outwards, using their fortune-telling skills to earn a living as they went. Some Gypsies read for the nobility and gentry, aristocracy and royalty in the courts of medieval Europe, others read for ordinary folk at the many fairs and festivals held throughout medieval Europe. Napoleon Bonaparte was known to be highly superstitious and fascinated by all forms of divination – perhaps it was his influence that gave these subjects respectability in 19th-century France. Certainly, the first books on 'scientific' palmistry emerged from France, the most famous of them written by Count Louis Hamon, better known by his pen name, Cheiro. Cheiro is pronounced 'Kai-ro' (or even 'Cairo'), and derives from the Greek word for hand.

The art of palm-reading can be traced back as far as the ancient Greeks.

Palm-readers can also divine information from the backs of hands.

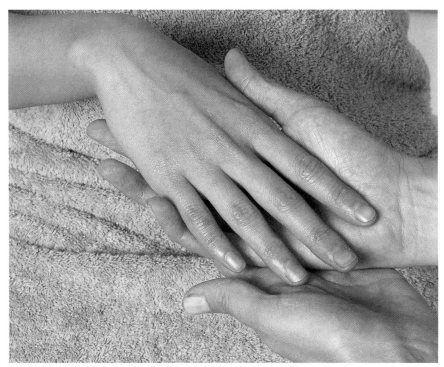

There are two ways of reading hands: clairvoyant or psychic palmistry and scientific palmistry. Psychic palmistry isn't really hand-reading at all because all that the psychic does is to take a person's hand and even peer into it in order to create a psychic link. From that point on, the 'reader' channels information in the same way as any other psychic. Scientific palmistry is the study of the hands, including the shape and formation of the hands, and the ability to observe and interpret the various aspects and features found there. There is no need, however, to choose one of these methods to the exclusion of the other – many extremely psychic people use a mixture of both – but even a reader who wishes to combine the two will need to start somewhere, and will need, at the very least, a basic knowledge of what the different lines and marks mean.

Hand-reading is a huge subject, so if you are to become proficient, you will need patience, a good memory, excellent powers of observation, time and experience. However, even a little knowledge can be useful, and can tell you an enormous amount about a person. I cannot teach you how to become psychic in a book like this, although I do include a small section that will help those of you who have psychic tendencies and wish to develop them. My book takes the scientific approach, which means that you can be as psychic as a brick and still make an excellent hand-reader. However, if you find your intuition developing as time goes along, don't push it away. So now turn the pages and learn what the shapes, lines and marks mean so that you can start to read your own, and your friends', hands for fun and for enlightenment.

NB: I have used the terms 'he' and 'him' in this book for the sake of simplicity. Naturally, the information relates to men and women alike, regardless of whether they are straight or gay.

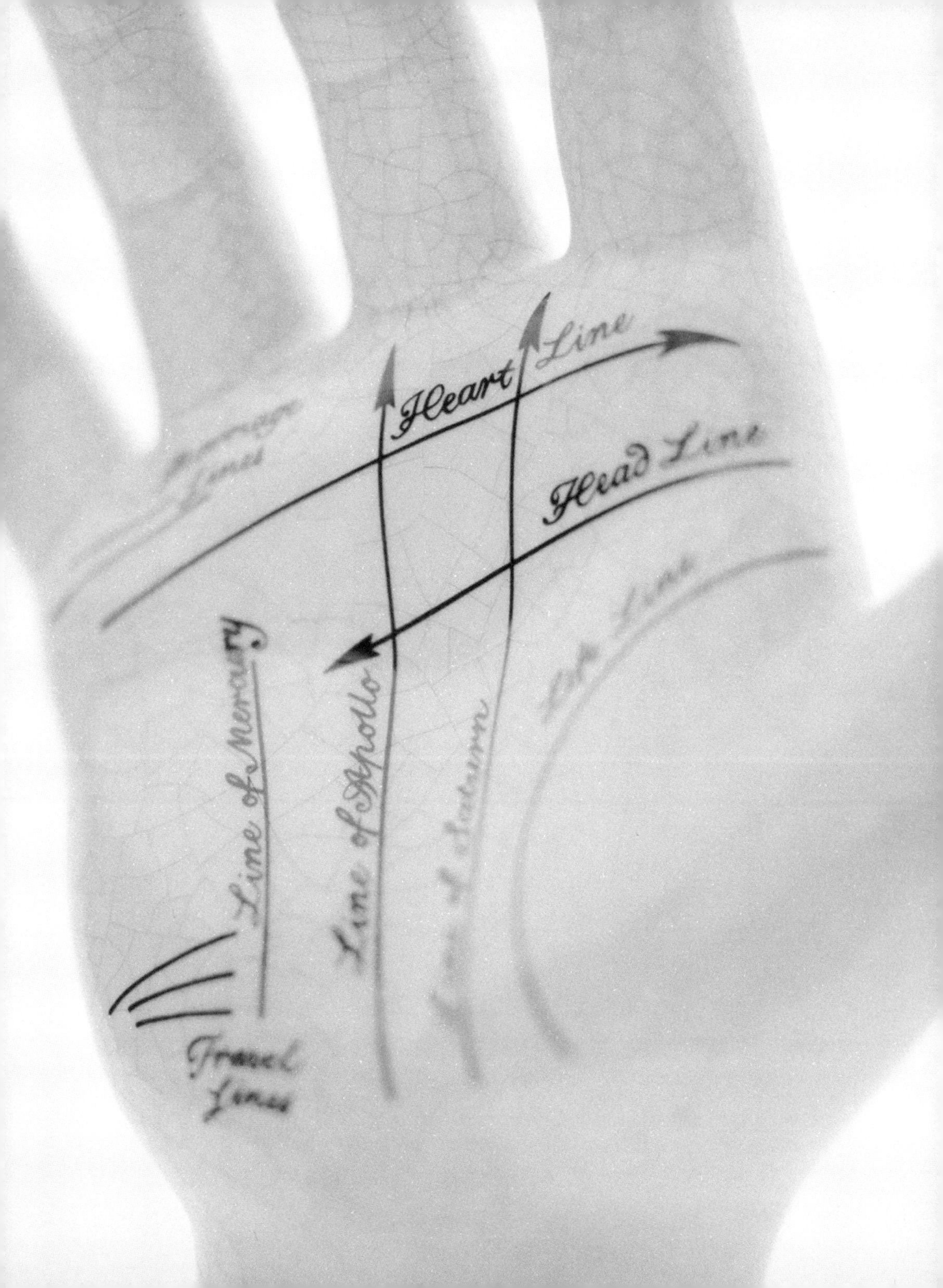

Heart Line
Head Line
Line of Mercury
Line of Apollo
Travel Lines

Observing hands

If you really wish to take a proper interest in palmistry,

start looking at hands wherever and whenever you can.

OBSERVING HANDS

Casually observe the hands of those whom you meet during the day at work or socially, and also watch the people you see on television and start trying to match the hand types with what you know of their personalities.

Only the other night, I was watching Charles Bronson in an old film that was being shown on the television, and was struck by how similar his hands were to those of my late husband, Tony Fenton. Not surprising, perhaps, because Charles Bronson was Tony's astrological twin, born on the same day and with almost exactly the same horoscope. Tony wasn't an actor, but he would have made a good one if he had wanted to. My second husband, Jan Budkowski, has hands that are totally different from Tony Fenton's, and his nature is also entirely different.

Now, let us consider all those things that you can see on a person's hands without making it obvious that you are studying them. You can observe some of the following aspects from across a room, but will need to be a little closer for the others. I have also included some general comments about hand-reading in this chapter.

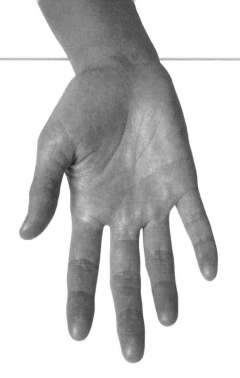
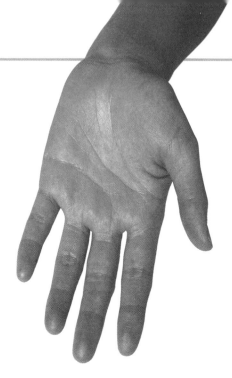

Which hand should you read?

A palmist always reads both hands. Science tells us that about 90 per cent of the population is right-handed, but, in reality, many people are a combination, and left-handed people are very often slightly ambidextrous due to living in a right-handed world. We usually consider the hand that someone writes with to be the dominant or major one. The minor hand is thought to show a person's inner nature and often carries memories of past events,

especially if they have been traumatic. Some palmists say that the minor hand shows what we were born with, while the major one shows how we adapt to changing circumstances. Some say that the minor hand shows the past and the major one the future, and others say that the minor hand shows the emotions, while the major one shows the practicalities of life. All of these statements have an element of truth in them, especially the one about the minor hand revealing more of the personal and emotional sides of life, which is why it is so important to read both hands.

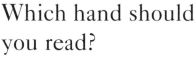

Radial and ulna

You may know that the bones in the arms are called the radius, ulna and humerus. The humerus is the bone that joins the shoulder to the elbow, the radius is the bone that links the elbow to the thumb side of the wrist and the ulna links the elbow to the outer side of the wrist. The radial side of the hand is the thumb side and the ulna side is what is termed the percussion side. Features on the radial side have more to do with worldly or abstract matters, while those on the ulna side are more concerned with feelings, imagination and relationships.

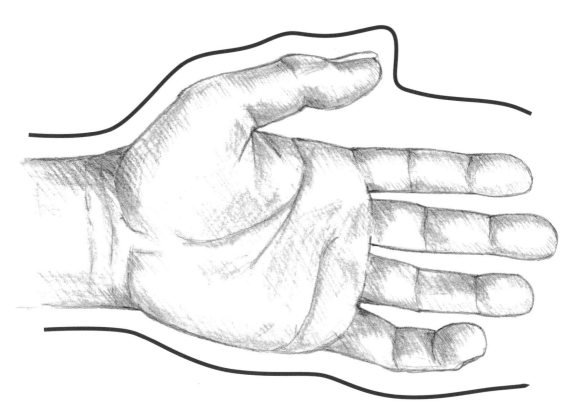

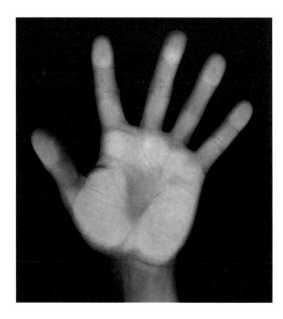

practical tasks than small ones. Small hands suggest an energetic personality who can see the wider picture and get new things off the ground, but he may have difficulty in coping with details or seeing things through.

Full and empty hands

Full hands are those with many lines and marks on them; empty ones have few lines. The person with the full hands tends to have a more nervous temperament than the more confident, empty-handed type. However, when trouble comes, the full-handed person can bend with the wind and adapt to new situations that would break the apparently more stable, empty-handed one. The full hand shows an active mind – sometimes one that won't switch off at all, while the empty hand shows a more practical approach to life.

Hand size

The hands should be in proportion to the size of a person's body, with small hands on a small person and large ones on a large person. In the case of any discrepancy between a person's hand and body size, consider the implications and see if there is anything slightly odd about it. The person with the larger hands can cope with details, but he may become so bogged down that he can't see the wider picture. Larger hands are more attuned to

Hand shapes and types

Cheiro suggested that there were seven hand shapes, and referred to them as elementary, square, spatulate, philosophic, conic, psychic and mixed.

Some of these hand shapes are obvious, but others are confusing to a beginner, and even to an experienced palmist, so I suggest that to start with, you restrict yourself to the more obvious shapes. A square hand denotes practicality. If any part of the hand is square, such as the palm or the fingertips, this indicates common sense and a talent for practical matters.

Long, narrow hands denote an artistic temperament, while those that have a rounded appearance suggest sociability and a need for variety in life.

Knobbly hands, with knotty knuckles, often belong to those who enjoy using their

The square hand.

brains and who are introverted, shy and slow to take action, while smooth hands suggest less thought and more action. Smooth skin on the hands signifies a more refined and sensitive nature than rough skin.

practical and responsible and partly dreamy, artistic or flighty. A square palm will add practicality to long fingers, while short, square fingers on a narrow hand help the subject to turn his dreams into action.

Heavy-looking hands denote physical strength, and if the hands are also fairly flexible, the person is likely to be athletic. Delicate hands suggest a more nervous and cautious personality, with less physical

The long, narrow hand.

Hands that have an angular appearance where the fingers splay out slightly at the tips are called spatulate. These people tend to be independent and inclined to live life their own way. They are clever and inventive, but they may also be quite lazy.

If the palm and the fingers don't match up, the personality is mixed, being partly

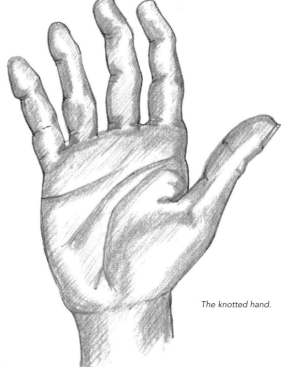

The knotted hand.

strength. Hard hands suggest a hard worker, while soft-handed types look for an easy life, possibly because the person tires easily. Soft hands can also signify pregnancy, hormonal problems, ill health and vegetarianism. Hands with hard-packed flesh belong to a leader who may be hard on himself, and he will certainly be hard on others.

The old-time palmistry books used to say that black hair on the back of the fingers and hands was a sign of a rough and uncouth person who might be violent. The truth is that some people just have hairy hands, and this doesn't mean anything special. When you can see the veins standing up on the backs of the hands, the subject is sensitive, possibly over-sensitive. No veins showing indicates a tougher and less sensitive or sympathetic personality type.

The heavy-looking hand.

Fingers

Flexible hands are said to denote a flexible personality, while rigid ones signify a more fixed type of subject.

Fingers that are rammed so closely together that no light can be seen between them signify a closed mind.

Fingers that fall away from other fingers suggest independence in the areas shown by the fingers in question. You will discover more about this later in the book, when we look at fingers more closely.

Those with fingertips that turn up tend to work with, or for, the benefit of the public and like helping others. Nurses and social workers or other agents often have such fingers.

Flexible fingers.

Fingers that are flexible at the base denote a person who loves to travel, whether for pleasure, business or both.

When the fingers are widely spaced at the base and splay out, the subject can't hang onto money. When allied to a short middle finger, the person might be a gambler.

A thumb that turns back at the tip suggests acting ability. This may become a career or a hobby or it may simply mean that the person is manipulative. This also shows an impulsive nature, such as the kind of person who goes into a shop to buy one thing and comes out with another, or someone who can take off into the blue at a moment's notice.

A thumb that is set low on a hand and that opens at a 90-degree angle or more belongs to an open and sociable person who enjoys working, and socialising, among others. When a thumb is set higher on the hand and lies closer to the hand, the subject is self-protective and will opt for a quiet life and possibly a job that he can do on his own. This person may be secretive or simply shy.

If the outside edge of the hand is thick and bows out sideways, the person will have a very short fuse and may be verbally or physically aggressive. If this area is thin and flat, the person will be timid and easily shocked.

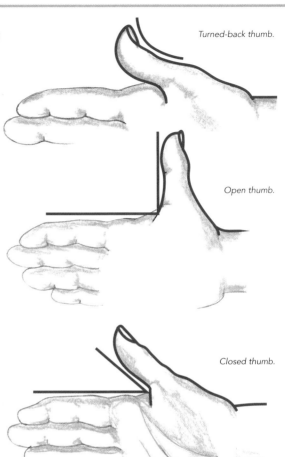

Turned-back thumb.

Open thumb.

Closed thumb.

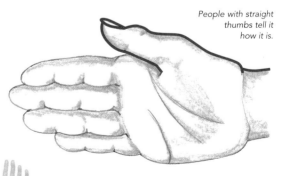

People with straight thumbs tell it how it is.

Colour

Taking racial differences into account, the relative colour of a person's hands is usually an indicator of their state of health at the time of the reading. Sometimes a patch of colour can indicate a specific difficulty concerning the health or emotional condition of the subject at the time of the reading. You will learn more about this in the health section later in the book.

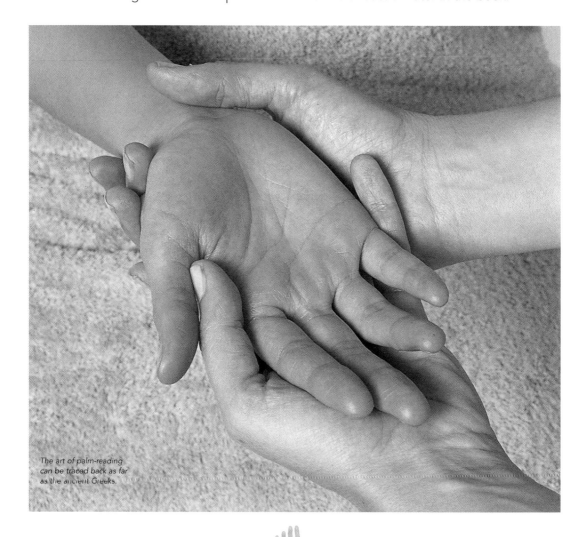

The art of palm-reading can be traced back as far as the ancient Greeks.

Basic rules of the game

Any part of a hand, any line and any feature may be longer, larger, wider or shorter, smaller and narrower than normal, so it makes sense to have some idea of

what 'normal' looks like. The only way to do this is to look at as many hands as you can until the idea begins to take shape in your mind. Remember, every human emotion, trait and activity can show on a hand, and any outstanding behavioural pattern will also appear.

Another basic rule is that any part of the hand that looks square in shape denotes

practicality, while any that are rounded denote sociability, humour and a need for variety. Pointed fingers usually denote sensitivity and idealism.

Watch the gestures that people make and see what they tell you about the person. For instance, a politician who lectures his audience by pointing and wagging his index finger is probably determined to have his say – and perhaps also his way.

We have now covered those elements that you can see across the office, or by watching someone sitting opposite you on a train or on television, so now read on for the details.

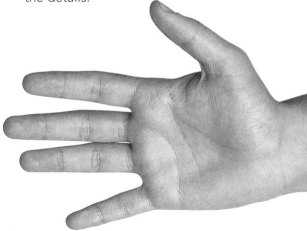

The map
of the hand

Looking at a hand is rather like reading a map – not

just any old road map, but the kind that surveys the

landscape and shows all the features on its terrain.

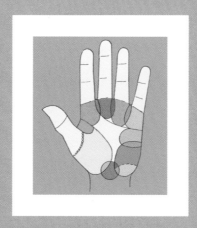

THE MAP OF THE HAND

Each part of the hand is associated with a particular attribute or interest in a person's life, and the marks, lines and other features on these various parts all have a tale to tell.

The old-time palmists who decided upon the layout of the hand map used terminology that meant something to them. Fortunately for us, they chose to adopt the names and the ideas behind them from astrology, and named the different parts of the hand after planets. As many palmists are also interested in astrology, this makes it easy for us to link the two and compare the ideas behind the two systems.

Some palmists take this even further by describing hands using the astrological elements of fire, earth, air and water types. As it happens, there are discrepancies between the two systems, so while a knowledge of basic astrology is helpful, it is

not absolutely necessary. If you wish to apply the idea of the elements, you could describe a smallish, energetic-looking hand as fire; a practical, square-shaped hand as earth; a long, bony hand as air; and a soft, gentle-looking hand as water.

The likelihood is that when these rules were first laid down, the two systems functioned in exactly the same ways, but as views about astrology and palmistry have changed over the years, discrepancies between the systems have crept in. The following gives a brief rundown of the planets as they are used in the two systems.

The map of the hand

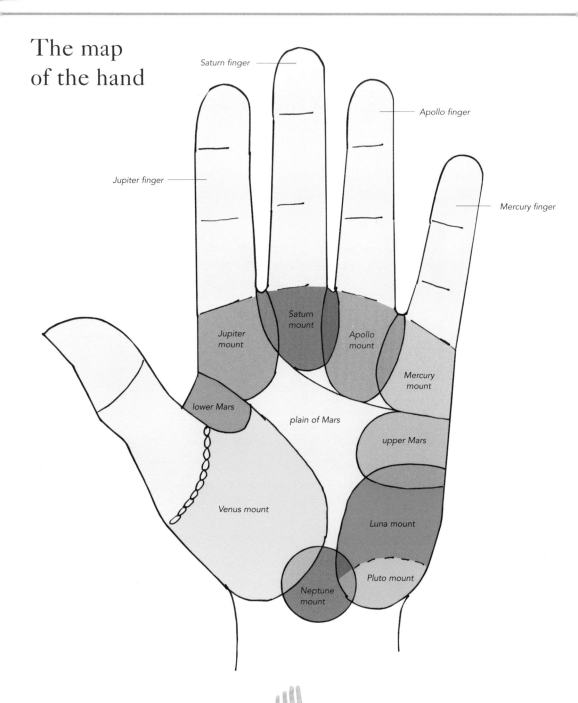

Saturn finger

Apollo finger

Jupiter finger

Mercury finger

Saturn mount

Jupiter mount

Apollo mount

Mercury mount

lower Mars

plain of Mars

upper Mars

Venus mount

Luna mount

Pluto mount

Neptune mount

ASTROLOGY

The Sun The ego, personality, business ability, love of children, creativity, leisure activities.

The Moon The inner person, the emotions, anything attached to motherhood and nurturing, the home and domestic matters, the public. Imagination, the unconcious mind and restlessness.

Mercury Communication, work, basic education, literacy and numeric skills, health, local matters, local travel, siblings.

Venus Luxury, possessions, ownership, money, love of beauty, love, passion.

Jupiter Belief, expansion of horizons, higher education, long-distance travel, foreigners, spirituality, legal matters.

Saturn Limitations, sickness, practical matters, hard work, structure, financial security, old age.

Mars Drive, assertion, aggression, energy, courage, military matters.

Uranus Originality, humanitarianism, democracy, education, unusual interests.

Neptune Dreams, imagination, psychic perception, artistry, creativity, escapism.

Pluto Transformation, destruction and rebirth, birth, death, sex, union, joint finances, shared resources.

PALMISTRY

Apollo The ego, personality, business ability, love of children, creativity, leisure activities.

Luna The imagination, travel and restlessness, creativity, the unconscious mind.

Mercury Communication, work, basic education, interests, literacy and numeracy skills, health, sexuality.

Venus Luxury, possessions, ownership, money, love of beauty, love, passion.

Mars Aggression and assertiveness, courage, enthusiasm, energy, military matters.

Jupiter Limitations, sickness, practical matters, hard work, structure, goals, aims and ambitions, old age.

Saturn Science, study, practical matters, hard work, structure, financial security, old age.

Uranus Not yet used in palmistry.

Neptune Imagination, psychic perception, the bridge between the conscious and unconscious mind.

Pluto Travel, escapism, restlessness.

Chinese palmists also produced maps of the hands, but these based the various areas of the hand on the trigrams of the I Ching, which were as familiar to Chinese occultists as astrology is to those on the subcontinent of India and to Westerners.

Most people think of hand-reading as a knowledge of the lines on the hand, and while the word 'palmistry' means just that, hand-reading as a whole is more comprehensive than this. However, either term is used nowadays, and palmistry is

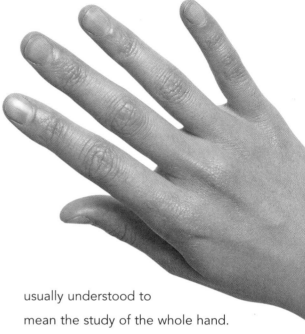

usually understood to mean the study of the whole hand.

Even the backs of the hands have something to say about a person, and there are palmists who have made a separate study of this. Gesture, or the way that hands fall naturally into shape, and even, in some cases, the way that people use their hands, are also important. I have mentioned gesture and some of these features, including some items that can be seen on the backs of the hands and on the fingernails, as a matter of course in this book.

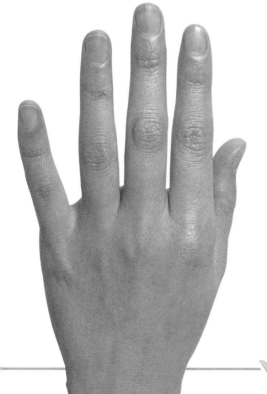

The fingers and thumb

Let's start by looking at the four fingers, ignoring the

thumb for the time being. Fingers come in all shapes

and sizes, and with a variety of tips and fingernails.

They can sway in different directions and their relative

length can be deceptive.

SETTING

The way that fingers are set on the palm can make them appear longer or shorter than they really are.

Fingers can be set on the palm sloping from the index finger to the little finger, in an arc or in a straight line, with either the Mercury or Jupiter finger dropping down. It is actually worth using a ruler when assessing the true length of one finger against the next to ascertain their true length.

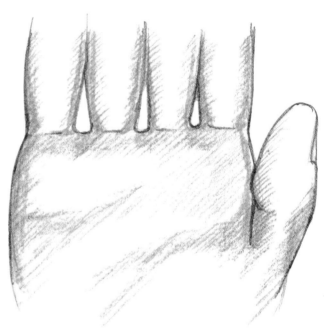

When fingers are in line, the top of the palm is obviously also straight, suggesting practicality. A creative, or possibly more sensitive, person has fingers arrayed in an arc setting, which denotes mental dexterity. Musical and artistic people sometimes have fingers set on a slope running downwards from the index finger to the little finger.

Fingers can be long, short, fat, thin, smooth or knotty. Short fingers denote physical

Fingers that are set in a straight line.

energy, while longer ones suggest a dreamy personality. Knotty knuckles on the fingers belong to a deep thinker who does things at his own pace, while smooth fingers signify less thought and speedier action.

Inclination

The outlines of the fingers in the illustration give a dramatic demonstration of how much the fingers can bend towards or away from each other.

Jupiter

A Jupiter finger that pulls away from the Saturn finger or bends outwards tells us that the subject likes to think and act independently, but if this is too strong a feature, it signifies a truly awkward personality who won't listen to others. If the Jupiter finger inclines towards the Saturn finger, the person is influenced by those who are around him. This subject is unsure of himself and needs the support and encouragement of others, but may be too easily influenced.

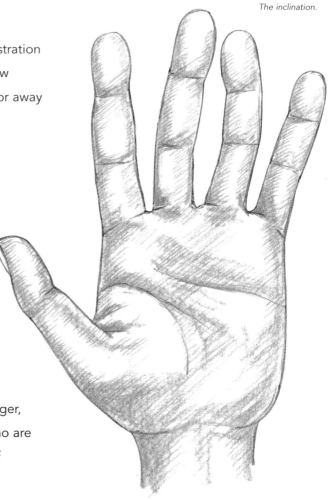

The inclination.

Saturn and Apollo

A 'V'-shaped gap between the Saturn and Apollo fingers denotes a rebel. My mother was interested in palmistry, and picked up some of her knowledge from Polish and Russian relatives who told her that this formation was well known among Bolsheviks and revolutionaries. I happen to be acquainted with a British politician who stood up for the ordinary people and the truth and was hounded out of her job as a result. She, too, has this 'V'-shaped gap between her Saturn and Apollo fingers.

If Saturn and Apollo cling together, the subject needs a job that gives him fulfilment and happiness. If he gets this, he enjoys working. This subject may not be

particularly conventional because he needs to work (Saturn) at something that he enjoys (Apollo). He tries to maintain a balance between family life, career and his belief system, and he often feels guilty when he fails in this endeavour.

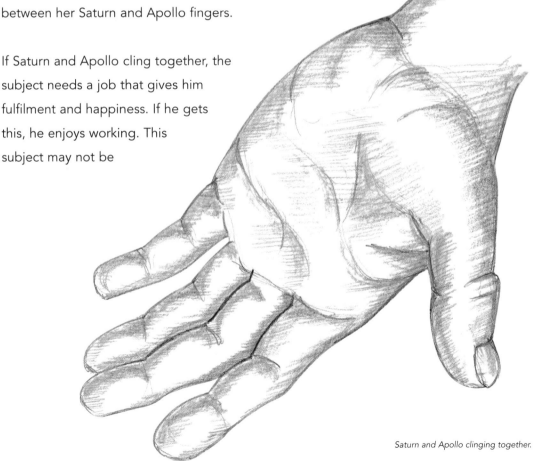

Saturn and Apollo clinging together.

Mercury

When the Mercury finger pulls away from the Apollo finger, the person is slow to commit himself to relationships and partnerships, but also slow to leave them once he has done so. Bends and kinks in this finger denote obstinacy.

Relaxed or tightly curled fingers

Look at the way that your subject holds his hands. This form of 'gesture' can change, depending upon how the subject feels at a particular point in time. Usually, the Mercury finger curls under most of all, followed by the Apollo finger, and then the Saturn finger, with the Jupiter finger being the straightest. Sometimes the Jupiter finger is curled more than the Saturn and Apollo, and in this case the person can lack confidence. This situation may be temporary, and as his sense of self-worth improves, his finger will straighten up. If the Apollo finger falls down below the others when the hand is relaxed, the person has family worries.

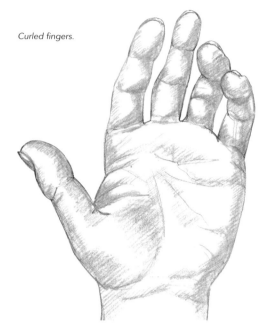

Curled fingers.

A gap between Mercury and Apollo.

THE KEY TO THE FINGERS

The Jupiter finger

The Jupiter finger is concerned with the ego, self-belief and self-motivation. It also includes belief in a god or any other kind of philosophy. It is concerned with leadership and the courage of one's convictions. The ability to go out into the world, get involved with politics or address the public for some purpose are all shown here.

One way of judging whether the Jupiter finger is long is when it is longer than the Apollo finger, but you will need to use a ruler to test this as simply looking at the hands will give a distorted measurement. When the Jupiter finger is long and well developed, the person believes in himself. He may also believe in a specific religion, ideology, philosophy or some other concept that gives him the right to state his opinions and supervise or rule others. This is emphasised if the fingerprint forms a whorl pattern or a radial loop. Strong-minded

Long Jupiter finger.

politicians like to wag the Jupiter finger around when lecturing others. When a palmist sees this, he knows that what the politician actually means is, 'My opinions are what counts around here!' In his personal life, this subject won't compromise or bend to the will of others, and he may be argumentative. This person usually lives and works among others, but he may end up leading them.

When this finger is short (e.g., shorter than Apollo), the person is likely to bend to the will of others and to fit in with the views of his spouse, bosses, teachers, peers or those around him. He may be a follower or he may quietly go his own way without bothering others, working alone and achieving success in his own way without controlling or organising others. He may prefer to be part of a homogenous group or part of a strong family group. He won't try to stand out in a crowd, and if he achieves stardom, he will try to avoid making others jealous of him because he cares about what others think of him.

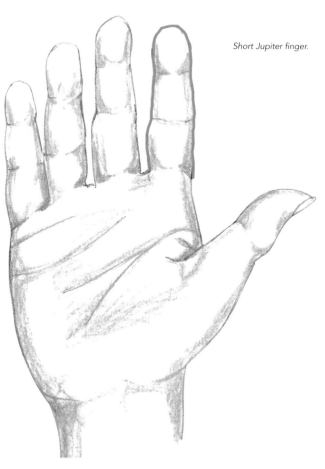

Short Jupiter finger.

Saturn

The Saturn finger is concerned with practicalities, finances and other such resources that are necessary for survival. It concerns the fabric of a person's home, in the sense of its value and security, rather than the life that goes on there. Saturn is also associated with science and mathematics and some aspects of business.

If this finger is long, the subject may choose to work as a scientist or in some highly technical field. His intellect will drive him. If Jupiter is also long, he will have strong religious or philosophical views, but he won't just stop at expounding these because he will be driven to work actively for whatever cause he believes in. This person doesn't spend money freely, and if the fingertip and nail are square, he will certainly know how many beans make five. A person with a long Saturn may be serious, dour or tight-fisted. Oddly enough, this subject may not be a hard worker, but

Long Saturn finger.

Short Saturn finger.

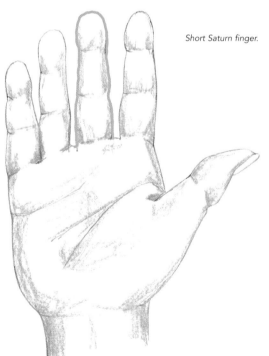

he will certainly have a good mind, and he may spend a good deal of time studying or thinking. He could be a good teacher.

When the Saturn finger is short, the subject may waste time and money. A short Saturn can sometimes indicate acting talent, which can lead to considerable success. Alternatively, he may be a gambler, confidence trickster or an honest and successful salesman.

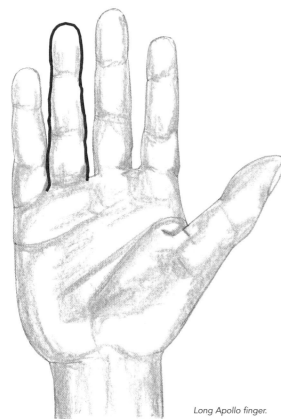

is sensitive and emotional. He may also be very sexy, due to the fact that his needs and feelings are close to the surface. He will be artistic, musical and creative. Love, family, a happy home and peace are important to this person. A short Apollo finger suggests that these finer and more enjoyable aspects of life are subordinate to worldly achievement, money, religion or other factors.

Long Apollo finger.

Apollo

This finger concerns home and family life, love and affection. Appreciation of the arts and music are shown here, as are all of the other finer and more enjoyable aspects of life. This is the finger of creativity. A long Apollo finger signifies a person who

Short Apollo finger.

Mercury

Long, straight Mercury finger.

This finger is concerned with communication in all of its forms. This can be speaking and writing, computing and working in fields that require communication, and also teaching and studying and business. Because sex is a form of communication, this is also shown on the Mercury finger. An interest in health and healing can be seen here, too. When the hand is closed, the tip of the little finger should reach the crease on the ring finger, but this depends upon the way that the fingers are set on the hand.

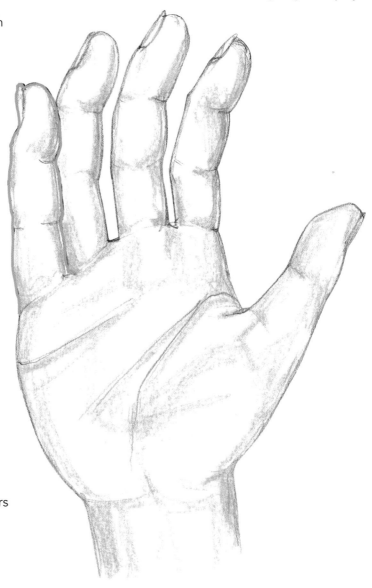

A long Mercury finger belongs to a good communicator who can put ideas into words, either verbally or on paper. This subject will make friends easily and will find and keep lovers due to his ability to talk, listen and sympathise. He will also be a sensitive lover because in palmistry, love and sex are linked to communication. A short Mercury finger makes it difficult for the subject to express himself. This may cause problems in connection with literacy, numeracy or sex. People with disabilities and those with brains that are dysfunctional tend to have short and oddly shaped Mercury fingers.

When this finger bends outwards, the subject is charming, but an inward bend may depict an argumentative or difficult personality. Both bends can suggest obstinacy. If the Mercury finger hooks, rather like the old idea of the polite way of holding a cup, the person can be absolutely bloody-minded. Little crease lines at the very base of the Mercury finger denote an aptitude for statistics, figure work and mathematics.

Bent Mercury finger.

FINGERTIPS

As with everything else in palmistry, square shapes indicate practicality.

A subject with square-shaped fingertips and fingernails has a practical nature and a lack of imagination. This subject may work with his hands or in a practical job – especially if the fingers are thick. If they are thin, he will have an aptitude for figure work.

Look at the fingernails and check whether the bases and tips of these are also square because this will emphasise the tendency to see everything in practical terms or in terms of black and white. If there is a discrepancy between the nail and fingertip, two different characteristics merge, as in the case of a creative cook, photographer or fashion designer.

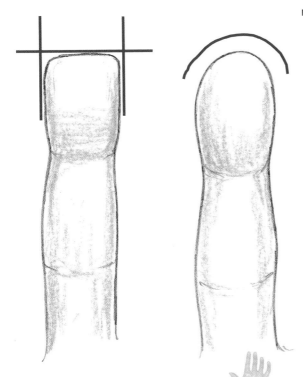

Rounded fingertips denote sociability and a need for variety in life. This subject gets on well with people and can be quite amusing company. He is generous and kind, but also a little lazy – or perhaps just laid-back. The best description for this person is: normal!

Pointed fingertips denote sensitivity and artistic talent, but this person sometimes finds life hard to cope with, especially if the pads of the fingers are also rather flat. This subject has strong beliefs and can be hard to influence. He is probably very moral and rather idealistic.

When the fingertips are spatulate, the person is very original, artistic and musical. He will also have a strong inner spiritual urge, and perhaps also a humanitarian one that will pervade all areas of his life. If you take note of actors on film and television, you will see that many of them have such fingertips.

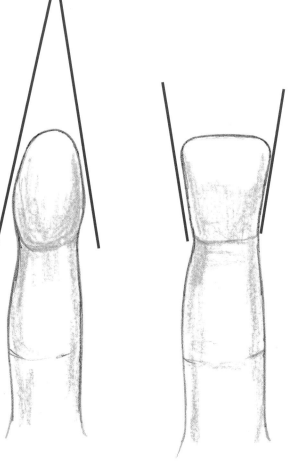

Both the pointed-finger and spatulate-finger types can be extremely successful in a creative or artistic endeavour, but can also be too dreamy to achieve much in life. Spatulate fingers can additionally suggest self-centredness or an argumentative personality.

Thick or thin fingertips

Thicker, heavier fingers imply less brainpower and more energy. These people are practical and can translate ideas into action. Thinner fingers imply intellectual energy, but less physical stamina, and these people may not translate their ideas into reality. Droplets or bulging ends belong to people who have a good eye for design and a strong sense of touch and feel. These people will run their hands over everything because they can almost 'see' with their fingers.

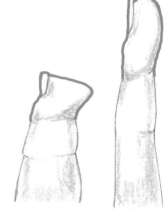

Fingernails

The rules for fingernails are similar to those for fingertips, which means that square nails denote practicality, while those that are rounded, especially at the base, denote sociability, generosity and friendliness. Narrow nails that show flesh on either side of the hand suggest sensitivity, vulnerability and a certain amount of caution. Wide nails can denote a harsh or bullying nature, and fan-shaped ones denote ambition and a lack of concern for the feelings of others. The nails are a terrific indicator of the health and emotional condition of a subject at any point in time. You will discover more about this topic in the section on health.

Fingerprints

The police use the same terminology for the fingerprints as hand-readers do. (I sometimes wonder whether any of the fingerprint experts also take an interest in palmistry.) The only fingerprint patterns that are likely to turn up on every finger are the loop and the whorl, with the loop being the most common print feature.

The arch

An arch, or even straight lines across a fingertip, are common features, but rarely show up on all of the fingers at once. The arch suggests that the person is rather ordinary, and that he will work hard

throughout life. The arch also shows that the subject lacks confidence, especially when this turns up on the Jupiter finger or the thumb.

The tented arch suggests fanaticism, and the finger that it appears on will show where this lies. The Jupiter finger suggests that the subject may be fanatical about a cause or some type of ideology. Tented arches can be seen on the hands of those who fall in love with someone and then hang on with all their might, even when the relationship ends. This is especially so when the tented arch is on Apollo or Mercury. Arches imply some area of self-induced emotional suffering, and they can also make the person tiresome to be with.

The arch.

The tented arch.

The ulna loop.

Loops denote a normal personality who likes variety in life and who enjoys the company of others. Loops are either called 'ulna loops', when they enter the finger from the outer side of the hand, or 'radial loops', when they enter from the thumb side. Ulna loops are common, while radial loops usually only occur on Jupiter or occasionally on Saturn. A radial loop on Jupiter suggests leadership qualities and bossiness. When on the Saturn finger, the subject is clever with his hands, and he may be a carpenter, metal-worker, jeweller, dressmaker or craftsman.

The radial loop.

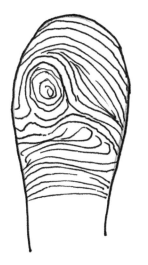

The whorl.

A whorl on the Jupiter finger denotes independence, determination, a go-getting attitude and selfishness in the area of life defined by the finger in question. However, a whorl on one or two fingers suggests talent in the area related to that finger. Whorls on all ten fingers either signify a real go-getter, a person who was born with a silver spoon in his mouth or someone who doesn't make any effort at all.

The peacock's eye is a less common pattern and it signifies talent. It usually turns up on the Apollo finger, which normally means artistic or musical talent, but possibly also a talent for home-making, craftwork or gardening. If on Mercury, it denotes a talent for oratory and writing. This person may also be an excellent counsellor, nurse or care assistant. A peacock's eye on the Saturn finger shows talent in a practical field like technical drawing, carpentry, engineering, building or civil engineering.

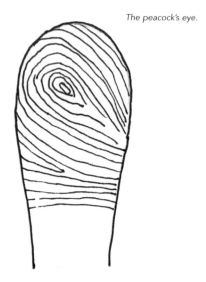

The peacock's eye.

The composite.

A 'composite' refers to a double loop or double whorl. This fairly uncommon pattern is rarely seen on more than one or two fingers at a time. This person has difficulty in making decisions because both logic and intuition operate, and these can sometimes confuse the issue. For instance, a person may look at a situation that seems perfectly reasonable from a logical point of view, but their intuition may simultaneously scream at them to avoid the situation – or vice versa.

THE PHALANGES

The words 'phalange' and 'phalanx' are related, but in palmistry we say 'phalange' and 'phalanges'.

The phalanges are the sections of the fingers between the creases that allow the fingers to bend at the joints. There are three phalanges on each finger, although some people may have two or four on the Mercury finger.

The top phalanges (the fingertips) are concerned with the way that a subject thinks. When these are long, the person has an active brain. A fat top phalange shows mental energy that may be put to some useful purpose, or it may be expended in arguments.

The middle phalanges show how the subject puts his thoughts into action. If these are long, he can act upon his ideas, but if they are very thin, he may think too much and act too little, and vice versa if these are especially thick.

The lower phalanges show the need for security and comfort, so if these are long, the subject will strive to make his life comfortable; if thick, he needs both financial and emotional security. Very thick and short lower phalanges may signify a person who eats more than he needs, possibly due to some inherited fear of starvation.

Two or four phalanges on the Mercury finger denote an unusual personality, and possibly an unusual outlook regarding sexual or financial matters. I once came across a charming guy who was an excellent cook and owned an interesting restaurant. He pursued everyone who might conceivably be induced to sleep with him, regardless of age, gender, race or background. I also once met someone with only two phalanges on this finger who was clever with money and also extremely stingy. The effect of this can go in a variety of directions, but the person will always be unusual.

Temporary lines on the fingers

Sometimes you will see little vertical creases on some, or all, of the phalanges. Unlike fingerprints or skin-ridge patterns, these come and go depending upon a person's state of mind or health. Many vertical creases signify that the person is overtired and probably overdoing things. Horizontal lines indicate that the person has more responsibilities than he can really cope with. When life improves, these lines disappear. Horizontal lines on the fingertips indicate a hormone imbalance or some kind of change in the level of hormones in the body.

The thumb

Many of the rules that apply to the fingers also apply to the thumb. For example, a square tip to the thumb indicates practicality, a rounded one denotes sociability, a pointed one shows a delicate and idealistic nature and a spatulate one suggests independence.

A strong-looking thumb denotes determination, strength of purpose and inner toughness. This subject is competitive. He may be a successful athlete, an entrepreneur, a pushy salesman or just a strong and powerful personality. A weak-looking thumb signifies a lack of stamina and a less competitive nature.

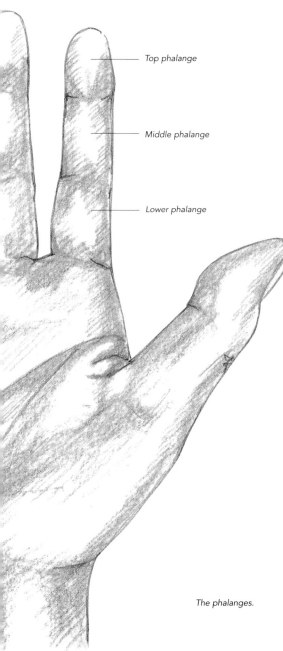

Top phalange

Middle phalange

Lower phalange

The phalanges.

Setting and inclination

When the thumb is set low on the hand, it will open out widely, and this belongs to an open personality. Conversely, a high-set thumb won't open out as widely, indicating shyness and generally a more private type of personality.

A person with a heavy knuckle joint at the base of the thumb needs a physical outlet, such as sports, athletics, dancing or working out in the gym. If the thumb is weaker, but the base knuckle is still prominent, he will be interested in these things as an observer rather than as a participant.

A subject with a high-set thumb who habitually tucks his thumb into his fingers is extremely very nervous. If a child does this, it is an indication of insecurity.

A flexible thumb that can easily be wagged around belongs on a person who is easily put upon or pushed around. Oddly enough, the muscles and ligaments around the base of the thumb become less flexible over time, suggesting that the person may become less likely to put up with bad behaviour from others as time goes on. A stiff thumb denotes someone who digs their heels in and who doesn't give way to others.

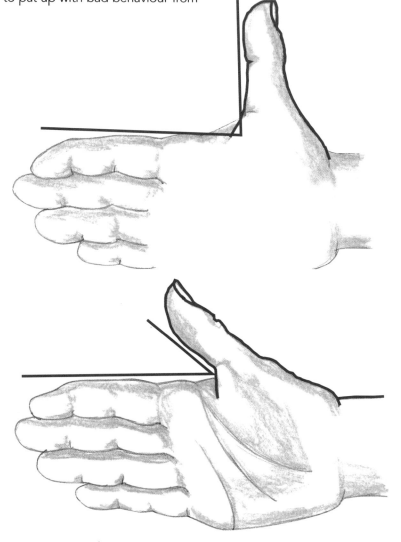

Widely opening thumb.

Narrowly opening thumb.

THE THUMB

The thumb is made up of two phalanges. When the ball-joint phalange dominates the thumb, the subject is strong-willed, energetic and determined.

Even if the thumb is not large, a healthy-looking ball joint indicates strength, willpower and determination. When this phalange is rounded and medium-sized, the person is co-operative and pleasant. When flat, the subject lacks physical strength and uses charm and adaptability to survive. He may bend over backwards in his desire for the approval of others when the thumb ball is extremely flat. If the nail side of this phalange is indented or spoon shaped, the person chisels away until he gets what he wants.

Stiff thumb.

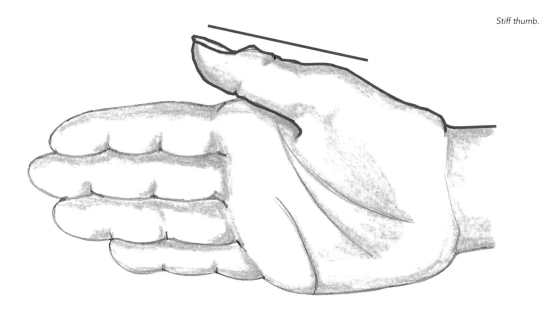

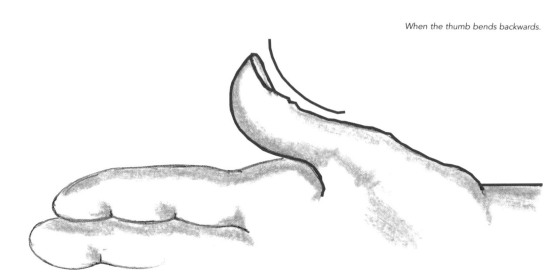

When the thumb bends backwards.

Sometimes the upper part of the thumb turns back, which is the sign of an actor or someone who puts on an act for a living or someone who may be able to manipulate others into believing anything that he says. This subject can be lazy or easily bored, but he is also impulsive. He will go into a shop to buy one thing and come out with something completely different. He likes to treat himself and, with a bit of luck, likes to treat others as well. If the second phalange is short, he may not think before he acts.

The prints on the thumb also follow the rules of palmistry, therefore, a whorl denotes willpower, determination and independence, while the loop denotes a normal, sociable character who enjoys being part of a team. The arch belongs to a hard worker who fears poverty, and the tented arch, to someone with a tendency to get upset over nothing. The peacock's eye is a rare formation on the thumb, but if present, it indicates talent, while the double loop suggests a combination of intuition, logic and psychic ability – and indecisiveness.

The second phalange is the phalange of logic. When long, the subject prefers to think before acting, and when short, he will act on instinct. A thin phalange of logic with a 'waist' or 'cinch' shape suggests a very logical mind and a real thinker, but also a person who wants to be liked. Lines across this phalange suggest fatigue and also an unstable home life or many changes of address or location. If life settles down, these lines may melt away.

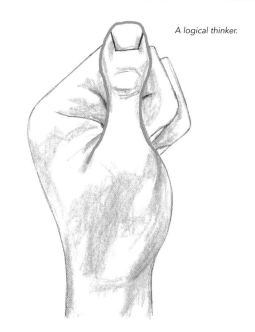

A logical thinker.

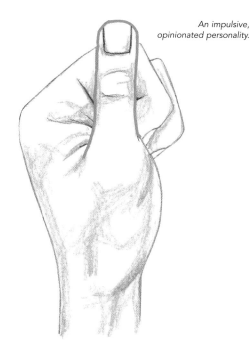

An impulsive, opinionated personality.

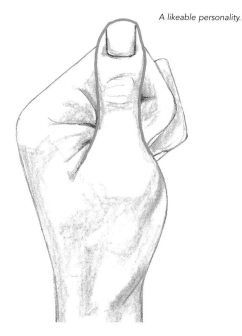

A likeable personality.

The mounts

The areas on the palm of a hand are traditionally

called mounts, despite the fact that some of these

look more like valleys.

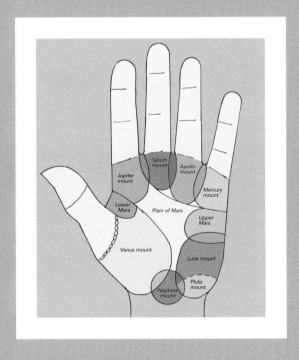

The mount of Jupiter

The mount of Jupiter is found under the Jupiter finger, and like the Jupiter finger, it relates to the ego and the subject's ability to make a success of himself. It also relates to honesty, wisdom and idealism. A moderate mount is needed here, but a high one can suggest self-interest and an overinflated ego. A flat one shows a lack of confidence. Thus the key to Jupiter is how the subject operates out in the world, and how he deals with people in general.

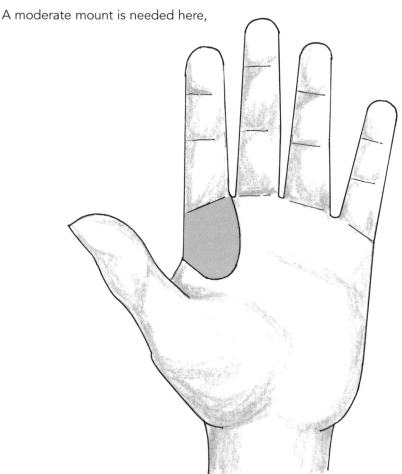

The mount of Jupiter.

The mount of Saturn

The Saturn area rarely forms a mount, although there may be a fleshy area between the Saturn and Apollo fingers. This indicates a certain sense of style and the ability to work hard at something creative. If this area is shallow, that is, if there is little space from the bottom of the fingers to the heart line, the person may be materialistic and unable to show affection, or even, possibly, to give love. The area is mainly concerned with practical matters, such as security, keeping a roof over one's head, money, resources and, to some extent, career and business, especially if this is scientific or technical. This shows the amount of financial and practical security that a person will have in later life.

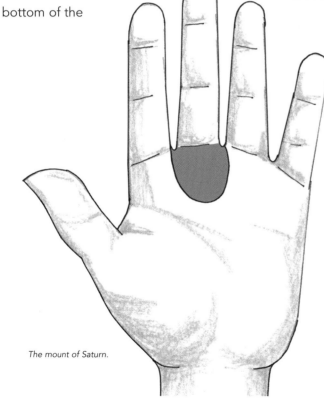

The mount of Saturn.

NB: An old superstition said that a person with a cross on the mount of Saturn would die on the scaffold, but don't worry if you have one of these because it is simply not true.

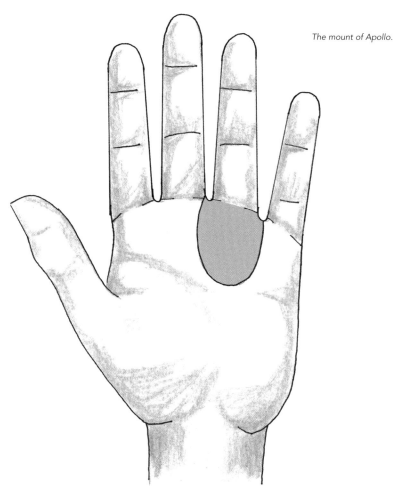

The mount of Apollo.

The mount of Apollo

Like the mount of Saturn, this is often more of a valley than a mount. If the area is cramped, the subject may be a sourpuss who can't enjoy himself or give pleasure to others. The area is concerned with home life, family matters, the arts and music and a desire to be happy and creative, and this shows the chances of happiness in later life.

The mount of Mercury

Mercury's is a definite mount, and if it is substantial in area and fairly full, the subject is intelligent and a good communicator. He may work with machinery and will communicate as part of his job. This area is also concerned with health and healing, and marks here indicate a talent for healing in some form.

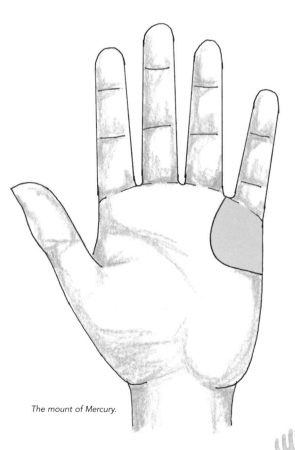

The mount of Mercury.

The mount of Venus

The mount of Venus relates to desire, passion and the 'feel-good factor'. Tradition tells us that a person with a large and prominent mount of Venus is sexy, but the truth is that while he may, or may not, be sexy, what he will be is passionate. He may actually be passionate about collecting art, music, the theatre, his home and family, gourmet food, travel, keeping horses or something else entirely. The passion is unlikely to be for a cause, a political or spiritual belief. These passions may be present, but they are not due to the size of the mount of Venus. Venus brings a desire for something that pleases the subject and that makes him happy and that can be considered a luxury. The passion is for beauty, possessions, ownership and luxury, and there may be possessiveness in connection with this person's desires. Like the thumb itself, a well-developed Venus endows a person with energy and determination, and it is often an indicator of worldly success, whether potential or real. Too pronounced a Venus can also indicate self-indulgence, greed, laziness, selfishness or too much sexuality and a jealous or bullying nature. If this person has the right combination of characteristics, he will make a great success of himself, but this desire to have what he wants and his laziness may be his downfall.

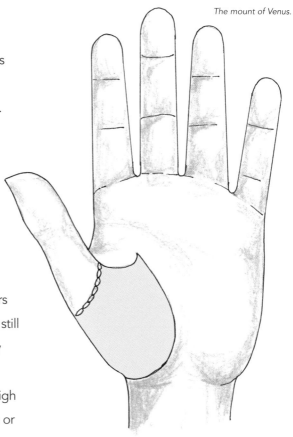

The mount of Venus.

A reasonable Venus offers zest for life, success in love and sex, plenty of admiration and affection. This subject has a passion for life, and possibly also for music, art, beautiful things and a nice home. He likes the best for himself, but is also generous enough to ensure that others share in the bounty. A flat mount of Venus still endows energy, as long as the area is fairly large. This subject is big-hearted and generous. Large Venus mounts, whether high or low, usually mean that the person earns or makes good money – mainly because he can't stand the thought of having to budget or do without the things that he likes.

If the mount is cramped, the subject may do without many of the benefits and trappings of wealth in favour of the freedom to be himself. He may be miserly and remote, with a preference for a spartan and lonely lifestyle. He may still be sociable, and even sexual, but likes to have a bolthole to scuttle back into when he has had a surfeit of stimulation and of people. This subject won't make an all-out effort to succeed in a career, and he may prefer an easier life or a quiet world of his own making.

Both large and small mounts can be seen on creative people, but the person with the large mount is more likely to make things that can be seen and handled. The person with the smaller mount will be more analytical, precise, logical, wordy and left-brain oriented.

Although we will deal with the lines later in this book, lines and creases on the mount of Venus indicate difficulties in obtaining the kind of money and goods that the person would like. Lines on the edge of the hand coming into the Venus area denote friendships or membership of groups, clubs, committees and social life.

It is surprising that this large area of the hand has relatively little information to offer. We know that large, small, high and low formations mean something, and we also know about shadow lines, median lines, influence lines and even parts of the life that stray into it, but it is still far less an area for study than other parts of the hand. I have a theory that this may tell us something about the specifics of the places that we choose to live in, the property and goods that we own and even the amount of money that we have to play with. However, nobody has looked into this to my knowledge, and my own research is a little too new to be published as yet. Perhaps it is a case of wait and see . . .

The mount of Luna

The mount of Luna is associated with travel, traditionally on, or over, the sea. It is also concerned with the imagination and creativity, and, to some extent, psychic talents. The ancients considered the moon restless because it travelled quickly across the sky, disappeared and turned up again during the course of each month. A large and prominent Luna signifies a restless person who enjoys travel and adventure. He may choose a career that takes him from place to place or he may travel for fun. Whether high or flat, a sizeable Luna always indicates a love of travel, days out and exploration of the countryside and the sea. A prominent Luna indicates imagination and possible creativity as a result of tapping into the imagination. Obviously, if this area is flat and cramped, the subject does not enjoy travel and he may not have much imagination either.

The connection to being psychic is really related to the imagination, this time in the form of the subject's intuition and sensitivity to surroundings and to images of the past and future picked up from people, objects or places. A high mount, or a whorl or loop in the skin-ridge pattern, or a specifically psychic kind of line, adds weight to this talent.

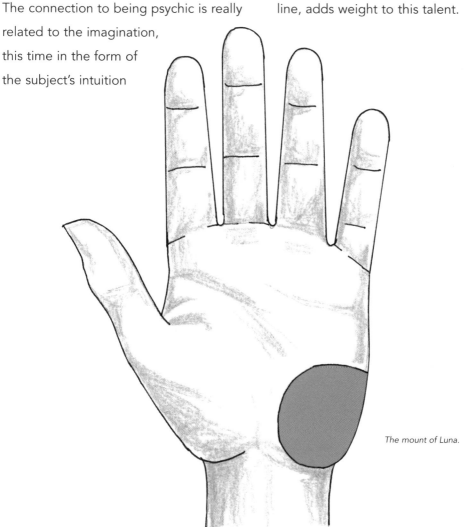

The mount of Luna.

The mount of Pluto

Right at the bottom of this mount is a bone, just above where the hand joins the wrist, and this area is now called the mount of Pluto. If high and wide, the person is very restless and a real traveller. If it is not prominent or low, and especially when it nicks inwards at the percussion edge, the subject may enjoy the occasional week's holiday, but really prefers to be at, or close to, home.

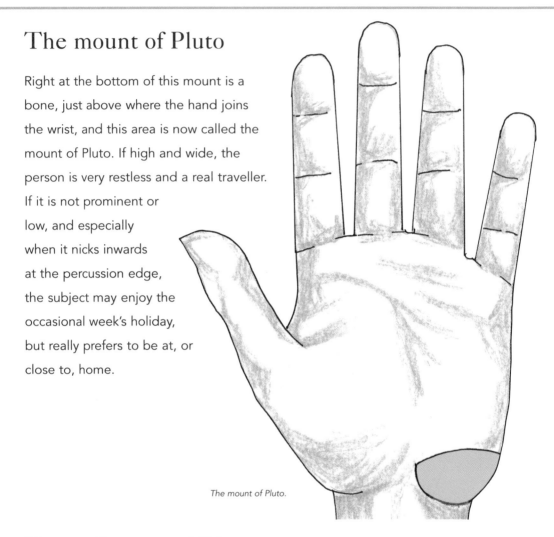

The mount of Pluto.

Venus, Luna and Pluto

The easiest way to think about these mounts is to consider Venus to be a love of people and those things that can be experienced with the five senses, and Luna/Pluto to be a love of travel and those things that are beyond the five senses.

The mount of Mars

Here things get a little complicated because although the whole of the central area of the hand is devoted to Mars, it is subdivided into upper Mars, lower Mars and the plain of Mars.

Upper Mars is located at the percussion edge of the hand and relates to fighting ability and such reactions as anger and belligerence. If this area is high, or if there is thickness through the hand, the person isn't easily taken by surprise. He may fight with words or with his fists, but he won't put up with anything that he doesn't like. This person may choose to serve in the armed forces, the police, as a paramilitary or as a paramedic, and he will enjoy being where the action is. Oddly enough, if this area bows outwards on the percussion edge, the person has an active creative talent and may work with his mind and hands in a creative manner.

If this area is thin, the person wouldn't volunteer to join the army or to stand on a picket line, and he may be nervous of people. This subject may have been put upon or bullied as a child, and remains somewhat cautious or nervous throughout

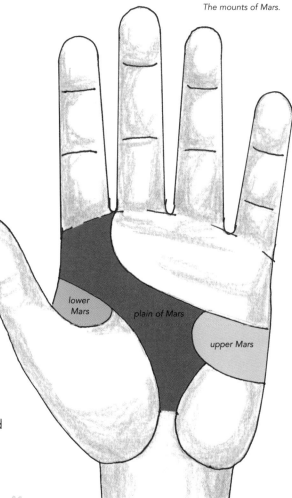

The mounts of Mars.

lower Mars

plain of Mars

upper Mars

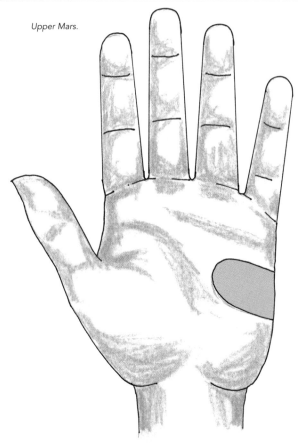

Upper Mars.

Lower Mars is often actually higher on the hand than upper Mars. Lower Mars is located on the hand and palm around and below the thumb opening away from the hand, and is inside the life line. Someone with a prominent, large or 'full' lower Mars mount can be counted on to do his duty. He is likely to have been a scout or a member of the boy's brigade, or something of that kind, as a child, and if he has to do any kind of military service, he will enjoy it. He is a good team member, especially if there is serious work to be done.

A flat, indented or cramped area here belongs to an individual who sees no need to join pressure groups or to get into uniform. He may be too much of an individualist to be a good team member.

The plain of Mars is the area in the centre of the hand. It has no meaning of its own, but this is where many of the lines of the hand cross.

life as a result. Check how the thumb is set and how the subject holds it for confirmation of this. If the edge of the hand is straight, rather than bowed, the subject could be a good record-keeper, secretary or analyst; he can interpret and improve upon the ideas of others, but he may not be creative in his own right.

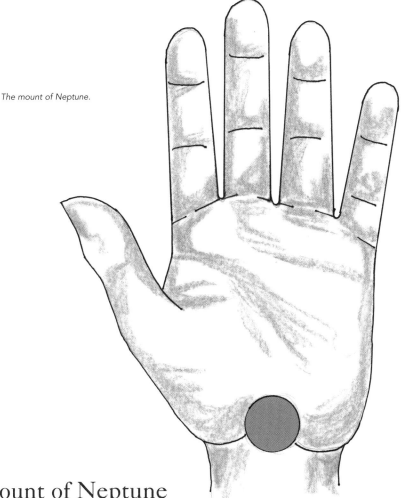

The mount of Neptune.

The mount of Neptune

Neptune represents a link between the conscious and unconscious mind, and also the spiritual and the material worlds. Psychics, spiritual mediums, artists, psychologists, dream analysts, creative people and those who travel have well-developed Neptune mounts. This links the material world of Venus with the imaginative or psychic world of Luna. It also links the conscious and unconscious mind.

Angles

The joint where the thumb meets the hand is called the angle of dexterity or the angle of rhythm. If it is reasonably well developed, the person has a certain gracefulness, rarely drops anything and is good with his hands. He also has a sense of timing, which is useful for music, rapping, dancing, sports or even for telling jokes. This subject has an instinctive feel for the right time to speak and the right time to clam up, and, indeed, for the right time to do anything.

The angle at the very base of the hand, where it meets the wrist on the thumb side, shows a love of music and melody. This subject may play an instrument or simply enjoy listening to music or dancing to it.

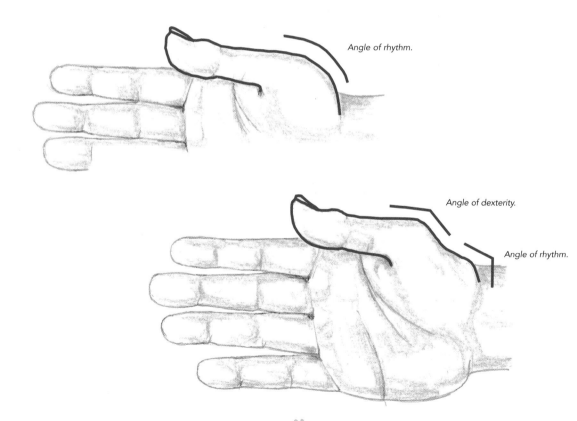

Angle of rhythm.

Angle of dexterity.

Angle of rhythm.

The lines
of the hand

Most people understand palmistry to be a matter

of reading the lines of the hand.

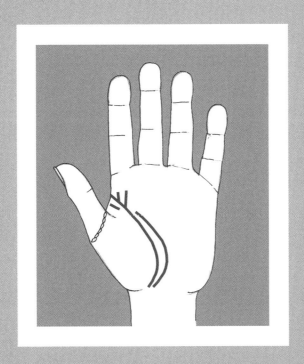

THE LINES OF THE HAND

As we have already seen, there is far more to hand-reading than this, but the lines are central to the subject, and anyone studying hand-reading should at least try to grasp the basics of this area.

Lines can, and do, change. Unless there is something radically wrong, a newborn baby may have wide or narrow, long or short hands, but the lines are much the same as those on any other baby. Later on, the individual formations grow and develop slowly throughout childhood and youth. As life goes on, increasing amounts of past data get recorded on the lines, but the minor lines and the endings of the major ones may still change later. Everything in palmistry is measured against a kind of average length, strength and design. Therefore, a line that is long or short, deeply marked or faint, in one piece or broken, unmarked or punctuated by interference helps to tell the hand-reader what is going on. Generally speaking, strong, deep lines show vigour and health, whereas weak or fine lines show a nervous disposition or weak health.

The three main lines are the life line, the head line and the heart line. An easy way to consider these is to think of the life line as showing how we live, the head line as showing how we think and work, and the heart line as showing how we feel. Any of these lines can be incomplete or made up of fragments that are displaced from their correct positions. This can make some hands hard to match with the illustrations in any palmistry book.

The fate line is important in that it is the main means of predicting events, but there are so many variations in the type of fate line that it is sometimes difficult to make any sense of it at all. In some cases, it is missing altogether. There are many minor lines that may, or may not, appear on a hand, so it is a case of checking to see what is present as much as what it actually looks like. An empty hand may show nothing other than the three main lines, which can make it hard to find much to say. A full hand may have so many fragments of lines and marks on it that it is equally difficult to read. The old-fashioned view was that a hand with few lines meant a calm and capable personality, while a hand with many lines indicated a more nervous personality. I have discovered that in some cases, the person with the empty hand is also pretty empty in other areas of his life, while other equally empty-handed people are quite neurotic and unable to cope with life half the time. A person with a full hand probably takes on too much, worries too much about loved ones, is just as neurotic as the totally empty-handed person and may be sick or weak in some

other way. The best kind of hand is one that has something on it, but not too much. It is true of everything in palmistry that the middle way is the best – or, as the Greeks say, *pan metron ariston*.

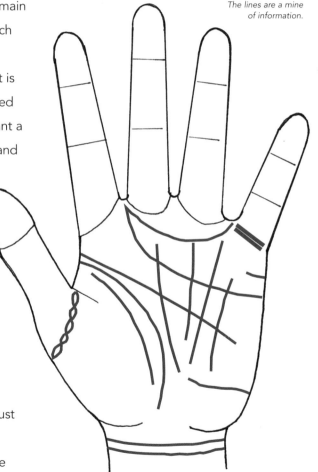

The lines are a mine of information.

The life line.

The life line

So let us now make a start by
looking at the life line, which is
concerned with the subject's
health, vigour and the main trends
of his life.

A long, strong life line is an indicator of
health and vitality, but as we will soon see,
a short life line doesn't necessarily indicate
a short life. The life line starts somewhere
above the thumb, heads towards the wrist
and ends somewhere down the hand.

A long life line that bows out into the hand
and forms a large Venus area indicates
passion and a desire to live life to the full. If
it is straighter and creates a smaller Venus

mount, the person is more of a thinker and
dreamer and less apt to put his energy into
making money. If the line rounds the base
of the thumb, then home life and the
trappings of a nice home and garden are
important. This person may strive to live
close to his work.

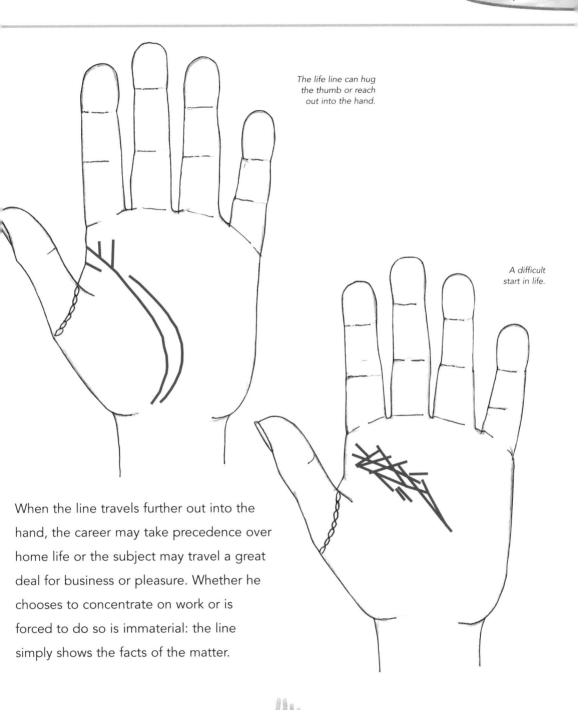

The life line can hug
the thumb or reach
out into the hand.

A difficult
start in life.

When the line travels further out into the
hand, the career may take precedence over
home life or the subject may travel a great
deal for business or pleasure. Whether he
chooses to concentrate on work or is
forced to do so is immaterial: the line
simply shows the facts of the matter.

The starting point of the life line

The life line can start high up on the hand, sometimes with a branch or two being thrown up to the mount of Jupiter, and this means idealism and a cool, logical personality. If it starts lower down, it suggests a more practical and sociable attitude and a more emotional and bubbly personality.

If the start of the line is messy, the person's early life was difficult. Islands here can indicate early health problems or emotional traumas. (Check the base of the fate line for confirmation.) A fine line that falls down from the life line in this area can denote the loss of a well-liked or loved family member through divorce, death or some other circumstance. A quick guide to the timing of youthful events is to drop an imaginary line down, from the middle of the

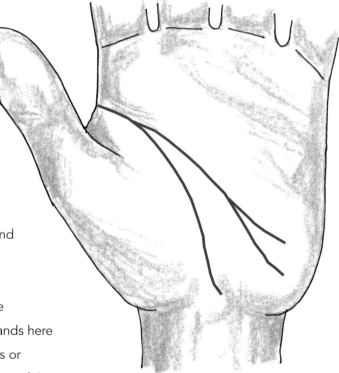

A traveller's hand.

Saturn finger, to the life line because the part of the line that precedes this point relates to approximately the first 18 to 21 years of life.

Forked lines

It is quite normal to see a wide fork at the end of the life line, which indicates that the subject is living a full life with equal emphasis on home life and the career. If one prong of the fork reaches out to Luna, and if the Luna and Pluto areas of the hand are well developed, travel will also be a feature of his life.

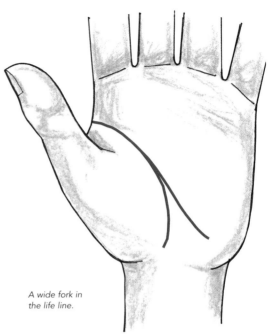

A wide fork in the life line.

A narrow fork in the life line.

A life line with a narrow fork indicates a struggle because the energies of the life line are split, suggesting that the person is trying to cope with two demands at once. A typical scenario is that of a woman who brings up children alone. This kind of fork will be so narrow that it almost becomes a double life line.

About the only thing that members of the general public think that they know about palmistry is that a short life line means a short life. They are totally wrong because the length of the life line bears no relation to the length of a person's life. Short life lines and those that blend with the fate line, or those that break and start again further down the hand, displaced to either the radial or ulna side, are extremely common. The chances of the person's life being cut short through illness or early death are extremely remote.

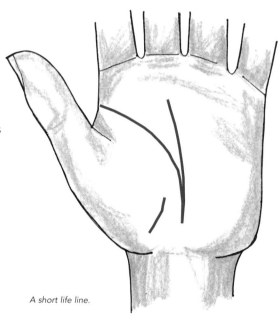

A short life line.

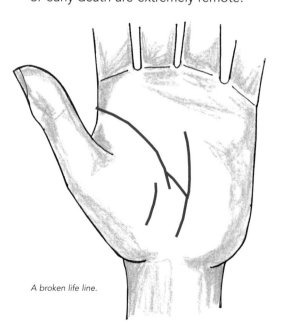

A broken life line.

I have lost two friends, one in his 30s and another in her 40s, to cancer, and both of them had long life lines. There are many variations on the theme of short or broken life lines, and these are not easy even for a palmist to interpret. The major cause is some sort of event that derails a person's life for a while, and this could be anything from a disastrous event to an extremely good one. Typical examples might be the break-up of a marriage or partnership, major job changes, moving from one country to another or important house moves. Even a win on the lottery can cause a short life line because it represents an event that changes the person's life. In some cases of a very short line on one hand, there may have been an illness or accident in the past that was potentially fatal.

Frequently, the line will start again further down the hand, or it may become part of the base of the fate line. In all cases, check for trauma, events and changes of direction. If a new piece of line lies towards the radial (thumb) side of the hand, this might suggest that a new home will be in the offing. If the line jumps outwards, towards the centre of the palm, the career

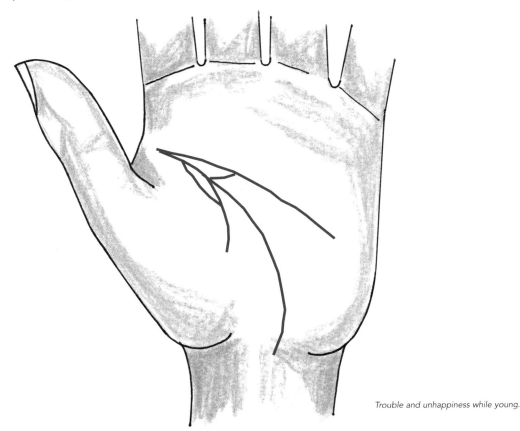

Trouble and unhappiness while young.

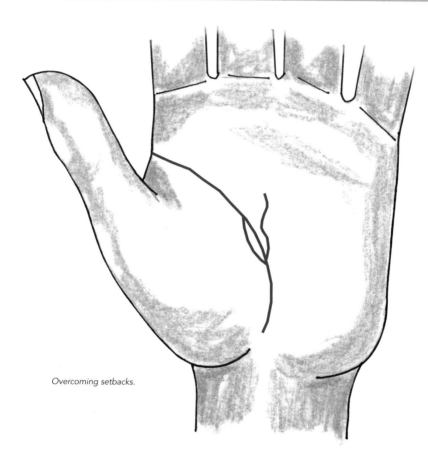

Overcoming setbacks.

will take greater precedence. If a new line appears that forms a fork, anything might be possible.

If you spot a break in a line, an island, a bar that cuts across it, or any other disturbance, make sure that you check out both hands because trauma will show up more strongly on the minor than the major hand, indicating that the event leaves an emotional impact. If such a mark is clearly shown on both hands, the subject's life will change in practical terms, as well as leaving him with bad memories, or there may be a health problem to overcome. A long, narrow island shows a period of deliberate self-sacrifice. This may mean setting aside personal pleasures for the sake of educating children or working while a partner studies or a subject who takes time away from work to study, which could mean being short of money for a while.

Lines that rise up from the life line show periods of self-motivation and effort. Note which mount these lines point towards as that will show you what the person is striving to achieve at that point in time. Lines that fall down show things that are given up or that have run their course. Very often an island is followed by a rising line, showing that the subject goes through a struggle and then makes a successful effort to overcome his problems.

Extra lines

In many cases, there will be a partial line that lies inside the life line. Different palmists call such lines the line of Mars, the median line, sister lines, shadow lines and so on. This kind of effect gives protection

from illness and accidents, and people with these lines are less inclined to fall sick or to catch viruses than those without them. This can also indicate spiritual protection or a spiritual pathway that leads the person into such interests as hand-reading, healing, clairvoyance and so on. Tiny pits on the life line tell us that something is wrong with the spine or its surrounding muscles, ligaments and tissues. Slipped discs and other such problems are a common cause. Pits that are close to the start of the line show that the neck is the problem area, while different parts of the spine are indicated as one moves down the line. Pits around the lower end of the line indicate problems with the hips and legs and the lumbar or sacral areas of the spine.

The end of the line

The life line may end abruptly, it may form tassels or it may just fizzle out. An abrupt ending suggests that the person will be strong and fit right up to the end of their life, while the other two scenarios signify failing health for some years before life ends.

It is wise to check the top of the hands, immediately beneath the fingers. Lines that reach towards the fingers suggest that the person is likely to have a long life. If there is nothing marked, it may be because the person is still young, so that these lines have yet to develop, or this may be an important health warning.

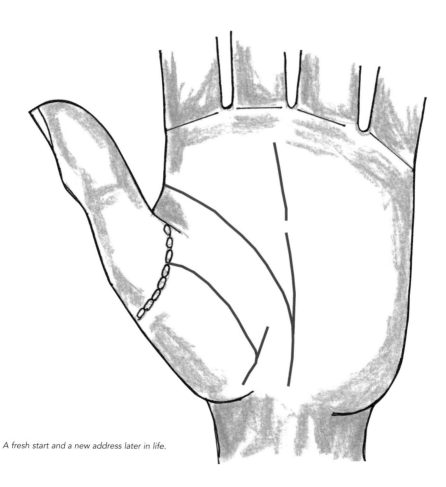

A fresh start and a new address later in life.

THE HEAD LINE

The head line is associated with the way that a person's mind works.

It can show educational and career developments (and setbacks), hobbies and interests and, to some extent, financial matters. The head line starts on the thumb side of the hand and travels more or less across the hand. The start and end points can vary enormously and still remain within normal tolerances. When the life line is weak, but the head line is strong, the person manages to overcome weak health or other problems.

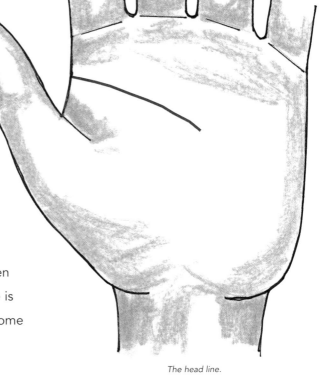

The head line.

Every palmistry book that I have ever seen says that a head line that is tied to the life line at the start indicates dependence upon the parents and an inability or refusal to grow up. This is not borne out by my experience as a palmist, and in practical terms, it can mean the exact opposite. A person with a tied head line will certainly be influenced by their parents, background, history and culture. This may mean that they marry into the same race or religion as their parents and family, partly, or wholly, for parental approval. The subject may actually leave home at a young age in order to escape a repressive, dictatorial or demanding family, but somehow the family voice still seems to echo inside the subject's head, disapproving and admonishing him at every step of the way. In some way, the person is still bound to the parents and may spend years either following the family line or rebelling against it. Either way, it will take a long time for him to find his own 'voice', philosophy and belief system. Sometimes there is a family history of tragedy, or a family farm or business or some other kind of dynastic situation that never quite leaves the consciousness of the subject. Sometimes it is his early schooling, or even a spell in the armed forces, that leaves an impression; sometimes it is war, exile or some other condition that remains in his consciousness. Whatever the reason, it takes many years for true mental independence to be achieved – if it ever does. Sometimes a tied line really does indicate a desire to remain tied to the apron strings, in addition to timidity and pessimism.

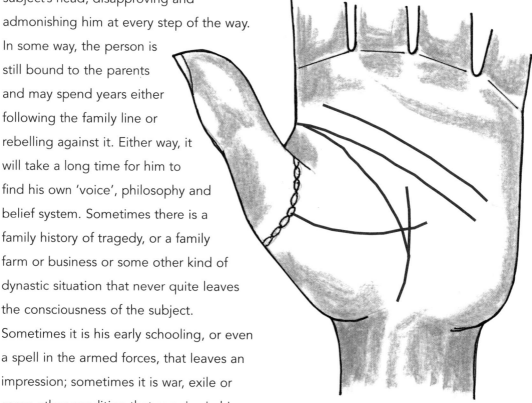

Tied and separated head lines.

The free head line shows that the parents and family have given enough approval and encouragement for the subject to become his own person, to obtain self-esteem and to act and think how he feels fit. This person may actually remain much closer to his family than the other type because there is no reason for him to do otherwise. (Check that the fingers also show independence, both in their length and in the way that they lean towards, or away from, each other.) This person is optimistic and outward-looking, and has the courage to do what is needed.

Cat's-cradle effect. Hatred of school or an unhappy home.

A muddled area that looks like knitting between the head and life line where they part either indicates that the subject hated school or that he loved it and used it to escape from a repressive family or early domestic difficulties.

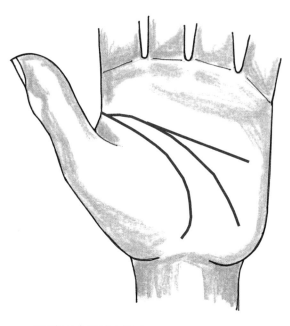

Straight or sloping head lines.

Straight, sloping and curved head lines

A straight line that travels across the hand denotes a logical mind and an aptitude for mathematics, science, computers, figure work, accountancy, engineering and similar practical skills. Success in business really needs at least some downward slope to the line because imagination is also needed for business success, and a truly straight line denotes a dearth of imagination and creativity. The subject may teach a specialised subject. (Check also for a high mount of Jupiter and longish Jupiter and Mercury fingers for teaching ability.)

When the line is straight and short, the subject is likely to be an expert on a particular subject, which he will bring into any conversation at any opportunity. It is difficult to give a reading of this kind of person because they will only understand what you tell them if you do so in black-and-white terms or in terms of their special subject. For instance, if the person is a pigeon-fancier, the only metaphors that you could use would be those associated with birds. If this is taken too far, the subject may be obsessive or paranoid. In my youth, the definition of this was a person who was convinced that he was Napoleon. I recently met a man who is the world's acknowledged expert on Napoleon, and who will lecture people on his hero at the drop of a hat. I haven't yet had a chance to look at his head line, but I bet it stops at Waterloo . . .

Another effect of a short head line is that the person can't be bothered to think or analyse anything at all and simply plods through life without making any mental effort.

A straight line that slopes downwards, towards Luna, belongs to someone who has a creative imagination. This subject can succeed in business because he can pool his practical, creative and imaginative skills and also introduce a useful touch of intuition.

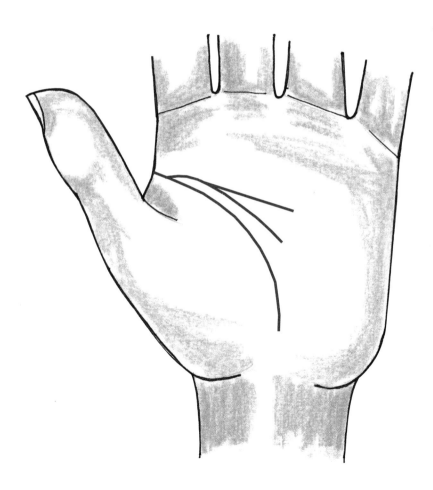

A straight line that suddenly dips downwards at the end belongs to a person who loses his temper or can be extremely sarcastic.

A long line signifies a person who never stops learning. If the line is straight, the person may confine his studies to his career needs, while if it slopes or curves, his tastes will be more diverse. If the line reaches the percussion, or if it touches other lines that do, this person may travel in connection with business or find work in new countries.

A curved or sloping head line that leans down, towards Luna, suggests imagination. This can reveal itself in the way that the person thinks, his educational and career choices and his intuition. He may be interested in travel and exploration or art and creativity, while if the line is forked,

he will have a talent for writing. If the line is long, the subject is discriminating and possibly a perfectionist. Curved lines indicate creativity, but also sensitivity, moodiness, depression and sometimes fear and terror. Some of this may be left behind from childhood experiences, sometimes the subject is simply oversensitive.

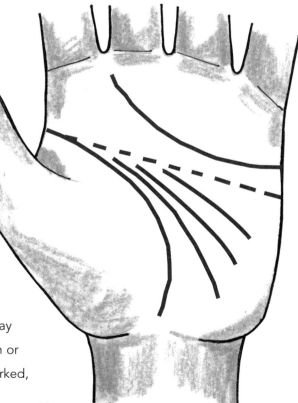

Head lines at different angles and slopes.

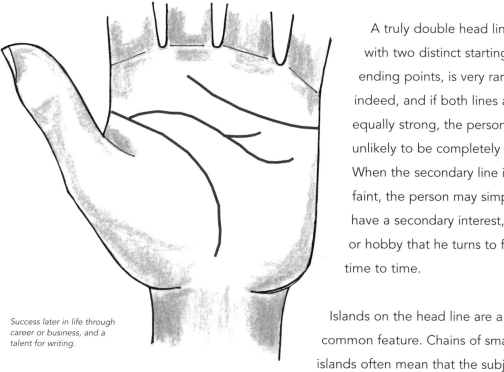

Success later in life through career or business, and a talent for writing.

A truly double head line, with two distinct starting and ending points, is very rare indeed, and if both lines are equally strong, the person is unlikely to be completely sane. When the secondary line is faint, the person may simply have a secondary interest, job or hobby that he turns to from time to time.

Variations on the head line

A head line that bends upwards, or that throws a little line upwards, shows that there is an improvement in the person's life, which is probably due to career or financial improvements. Downward bends and falling lines can indicate losses, but they can also denote jobs or interests that are discarded for some reason.

Islands on the head line are a common feature. Chains of small islands often mean that the subject suffers from headaches. An isolated island indicates a career or educational setback, a financial setback or unhappiness at work. Often, this accompanies a feeling of being imprisoned in the wrong job, the wrong marriage or the wrong lifestyle. If the island forms a triangle or diamond, it can mean actual imprisonment. A really deep island that splits the head line into two for part of its journey and then rejoins it can denote mental illness.

NB: A small island under Saturn can indicate deafness, or, under Apollo, eye problems. A series of small islands that looks like a skein of wool shows migraine.

A fork on the head line is often called the writer's fork, and it is said to show a talent for oratory or writing. (Check small lines flowing from the head or fate line towards the mount of Mercury.) Forks also imply versatility and varied interests. A subject with two different part-time jobs or a hobby or spare-time activity that is very different from his day job will display such forks. Often, this person does something ordinary for a living, but is keen on something creative, expressive or artistic in his spare time. I have seen this on the hand of an accountant who was also a competition ballroom dancer, a banker who was also an astrologer, a plumber who was a numerologist, a taxi driver who was a palaeontologist, an electrician who was a healer and a housewife who did something secret for MI5!

Breaks in the head line are common, and they may indicate a career break or even a period away from normal life due to sickness – especially if this affects anything in, or around, the head area. If there is a break with a square mark around it, the subject will make a full recovery. Long lines that wander across the hand indicate interference in the person's education, career or life. If these come from inside the life line, the family will interfere. Short bars indicate short, sharp setbacks.

Too many forks, branches, tassels, islands, breaks and other disturbances are an indication of a troubled mind or a lifetime of struggle. If the head line is in pieces, it is hard for the subject to get his act together. A tassel ending is not a good omen as it indicates possible Parkinson's disease or Alzheimer's disease in later life.

THE HEART LINE

While the life line shows how we live, and the head line shows how we think and work, the heart line shows how we feel.

It would be nice if this line showed the progress of a person's love life in detail because this is what the majority of clients want information about, but, unfortunately, the heart line offers no more than some tantalising glimpses.

Heart lines can be deep or shallow, long or short, clear or full of marks, islands, flakes and interference. The firmer the heart line, the happier the love life. A person with a firm, clear heart line may never question his self-worth because he receives plenty of love and attention from his parents and his partner. Oddly enough, this person may not be as loved as he feels himself to be because he may be blissfully unaware of how his actions irritate or hurt his partner. On the other hand, he may simply be an excellent relater who is also extremely lucky in love.

Young people often have very flaky or disturbed lines, which settle down as they grow older. This can be due to dietary, or even hormonal, problems.

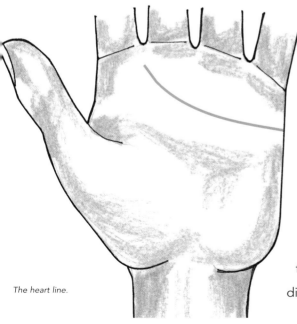

The heart line.

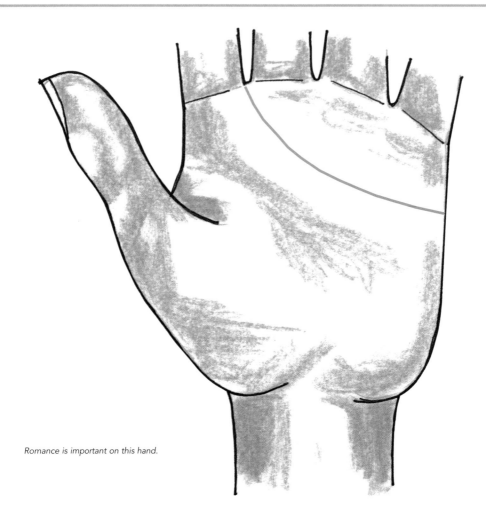

Romance is important on this hand.

Where to start

Some palmists consider that the heart line starts at the percussion edge of the hand, while others see the end that is closer to the thumb side as the starting point. To be honest, it does not matter that much because it is almost impossible to time events on this line. I have always called the percussion end the start of this line, so that is how I refer to it in this book.

A long heart line shows a capacity for affection and friendship, while a short one shows an inward-looking nature that finds it hard to understand the meaning of love or hard to be a really good and reliable friend to others. Such a person may be selfish, unreasonable or unable to give their heart to another.

A curved heart line shows a capacity for affection and love, and this subject is interested in the needs of others, as well as his own. He probably loves children, animals and his family. This subject wants to be loved in return for the love that he gives to others. If a relationship breaks up, he will suffer, but he will get over it in time and move on to love and trust the next person. Articles in magazines that describe some horrifying life story and then end it by saying, 'So-and-so has now found love with a new partner and has put the past behind him (or her)', are talking about a person with a curved heart line.

When the line is long and curved, the subject is likely to fall in love with someone who he feels understands him. This subject won't be influenced in his choice of partner by any other consideration than the fact that the lover feels right. Parental and other disapproval don't come into the picture because this subject simply has to follow his heart. If you saw the film *Pretty Woman*, with Richard Gere and Julia Roberts, you will get the idea. Clearly, a patrician businessman and a prostitute are not a match that anyone in his (or possibly her) circle could approve of, but the idea is that love conquers all. The person with the curved heart line is romantic, and probably headstrong and impulsive as well, and will definitely put his feelings before any other consideration.

A straight heart line shows a picky or choosy attitude and a person who uses some kind of calculation when choosing a partner. The partner must come into some kind of preconceived category. Perhaps the right kind of education, cultural or racial background, class, the same financial group or some other kind of advantage. This isn't

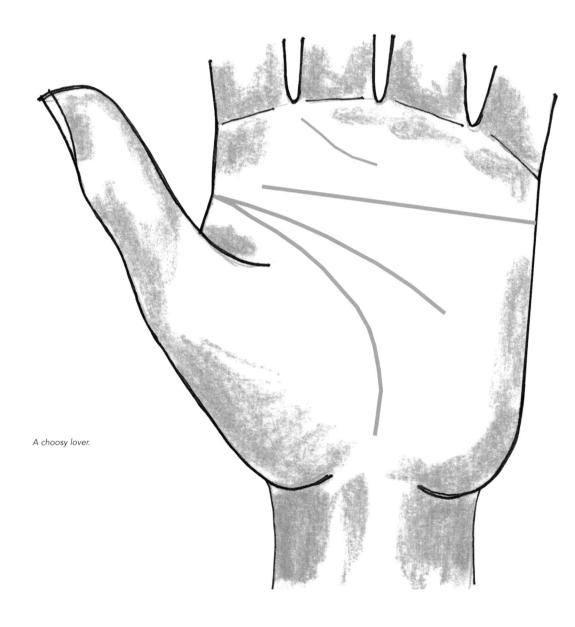

A choosy lover.

to say that the choice is deliberately calculated, but simply that there is a filter in the subject's mind that automatically rejects the 'unsuitable' person. Sometimes there is a sexual preference for a certain race or type. I remember one friend of mine with a very straight heart line. He was born two streets away from Sean Connery in Edinburgh, and looked and sounded much like Connery. His taste was exclusively for black women. This was just as much an issue as the person who will only choose a partner that he can take home to mother in the knowledge of meeting her full approval. Such factors as the religion of future children could affect this person's choice of spouse or life partner. Such a person may be happy to have a fling with an unsuitable person, but he won't want to introduce them to his family.

I knew one man with a strong, straight line who had done the 'right thing' in his first marriage and had chosen a wife from the same background as his family. This was partly because he felt that he could only be happy in such circumstances and partly for the sake of future children. Eventually his wife died, his parents were long gone and he was past wanting to have children, so he was finally able to explore other options. His next three partners were women who came from distant parts of the world and from different races, religions and cultures than those of his family. The built-in calculation of the heart line still applied, though, because he loved travel and living in exotic locations.

A shallow heart line suggests less ability to love or someone who wants to love and be loved, but never quite manages it successfully.

However, having said all of the above, a deep heart line that dips down, close to the head line, can be a sign of intolerance. This person may be demanding, fussy, a perfectionist or full of rules and regulations about how life should be lived.

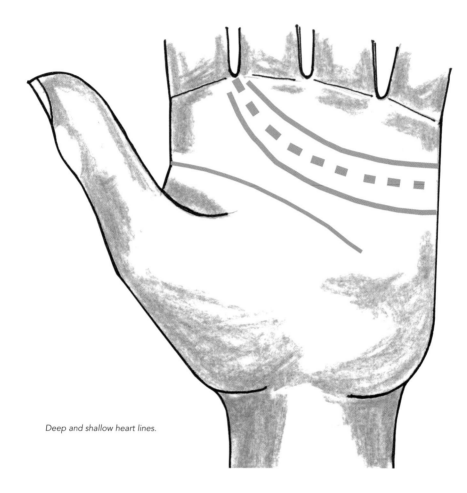

Deep and shallow heart lines.

Disturbed heart lines

A person with a fragmented heart line may be more successful as a friend than in a permanent relationship.

Breaks in the heart line indicate relationship break-ups or even heartbreak. Islands also mean times of emotional trouble. Sometimes, a clear island under the Apollo finger signifies that a relationship ended suddenly, and with a shock. In some cases, this is due to the sudden death of a partner, and in others, it is because the partner walks out without giving any warning signs.

Breaks are often followed by a new piece of line, although this may be displaced above, below or somewhat diagonal to the original line. Any fresh piece of line signifies a new relationship. Even if the line is a mess, but there is a new piece of line that reaches upwards, towards the fingers, the person will find love later in life. If a tiny, doubled line reaches to the gap between the Jupiter and Saturn fingers, this is definitely the case.

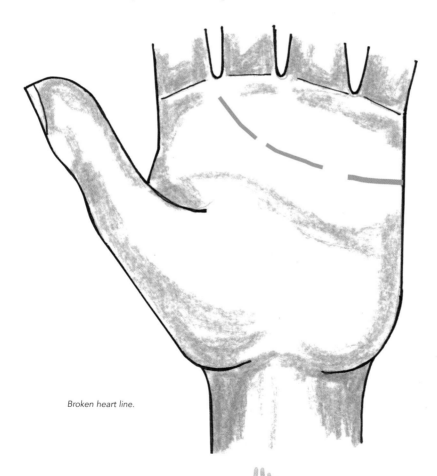

Broken heart line.

Friendships

We see love in terms of romantic and sexual love, passion, soul mates and mating or the modern equivalent of marriage. However, there are many forms of love that don't involve sex, including the love of one's parents, children, friends and pets, so a strong-looking line shows a capacity for all forms of love.

A person with a straight heart line that curves downwards, or that throws a heavy line downwards towards the start of the head and life line, is connected to the past and to his parents in some way. This may be due to deep love or to unpleasant childhood experiences, but the end result is that the past impinges on the present and the future.

Many people have light lines that fork and fall downwards from the latter stages of the heart line, and these simply indicate friendships. Other forks show that the person can be a friend, a lover and a companion, depending upon the circumstances of his life.

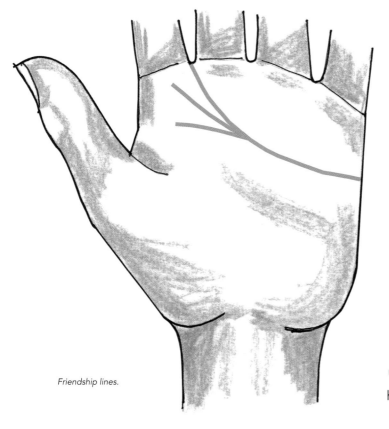

Friendship lines.

The so-called 'mystic cross'

In my earlier days as a palmist, clients sometimes used to shove a hand out at me and tell me proudly that they had a so-called 'mystic cross' on their palm. These people had obviously read the books written by Cheiro in the 19th century, or those of other writers who copied his ideas. If this cross exists, it is located between the heart and head line, and it has to be completely independent and not touching any other line. This is supposed to indicate clairvoyance. I can't recall ever seeing this cross, but I know plenty of clairvoyants, channellers, mediums and psychics.

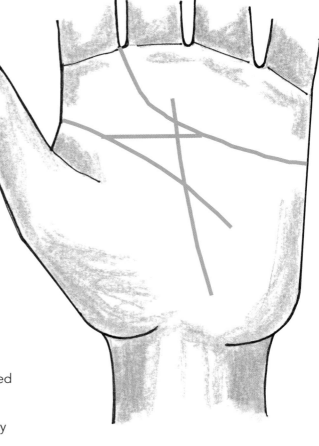

The so-called 'mystic cross'.

Something that is common is a line that runs almost horizontally, or on a slight slant, from the heart line to the head line. When this crosses the fate line (as it often does), the subject will find that their lover leaves them for no apparent reason, and this is due to a lack of any real communication or understanding between the partners.

Health on the heart line

Islands on the heart line can indicate eye problems, dental problems, lung problems, breast problems and many other conditions. Any serious disturbance on an otherwise fairly clear line suggests health problems. A spiky, tasselled or messy start to the heart line (the percussion end) indicates problems with the myocardium or arteries (also check the colour of the nails and fingers). Blueish pits on the line in the areas below and between Saturn and Mercury can indicate lung problems, while disturbances between Saturn and Jupiter can indicate breast problems.

No heart line or variations on a theme

Sometimes there is no real heart line. There may be a partial line at the start that fizzles out, and this indicates a relationship that should have come to something, but that fell apart. If there is a partial line at the other end, the person will have ups and downs in his love life, but will be happy later on. If there is a line in the middle, but not at the start or finish, the road to true love will be a bit rocky – it also signifies a kind heart and a sense of humour.

A final thought

There is no difference between the heart line of a straight person and that of a gay person, unless the subject suffers major mental anguish or major family problems due to their sexual preferences. In this case, the line may throw a strong branch down into the area where the head and life lines start.

The wrong use of love, as in sexual abuse by a family member, will have the same effect on a hand. Sometimes a parent rejects a child that they feel sexually drawn to without admitting even to themselves why they are pushing the child away. In cases such as these, the heart line throws a strong branch, or even twists itself down, to the area where the head and life lines are starting their journey.

SIMIAN AND SEMI-SIMIAN LINES

If you look at the map of the hand at the beginning of this book, you will see the standard formation, with the heart line running under the fingers, the head line sloping across and down, the life line around the mount of Venus and the fate line running faintly up the middle.

This basic layout is said to form a lucky 'M', which comes about when these major lines form this shape. This may be the standard formation, but a huge variety of other forms occur, and one that is seen in the hands of about 15 per cent of the population is the simian line.

The simian line is often heavy, with a chained formation. It cuts right across the hand, and there may be absolutely no head or heart line at all. In many cases, there are what we call 'semi-simian' formations, where there are vestigial pieces of the head and heart line left on the hand.

The word 'simian' means 'monkey-like', and

it was thought that monkeys had this formation on their hands. Being dedicated to my job, I have visited zoos and studied the hands of many apes and monkeys, even going as far as taking the handprints of a baby Barbary ape when I was in

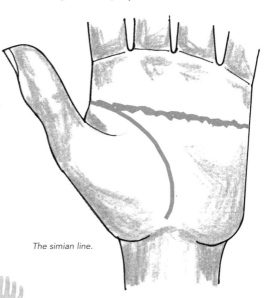

The simian line.

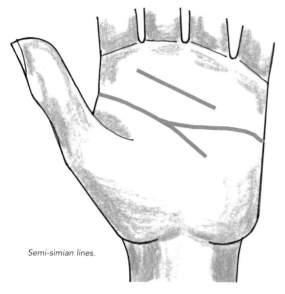

Semi-simian lines.

Gibraltar. The upshot of my investigations is that the lines on any monkey or ape hand are the same as normal human ones. The skin-ridge patterns are quite different as there are more of them, they are strongly marked and they appear in places where humans don't have them.

Those who have such lines find it difficult to lead a normal, balanced kind of life. This person may be a workaholic who ignores the private side of life, or he could be so consumed by matters of love that he ignores his work. These people find their emotions hard to deal with. They hold everything in for too long, allowing resentment to build up, and then either explode in a tantrum or in floods of tears. This behaviour is often confusing and frightening for a partner or children, especially as it can come out of the blue. These people could probably benefit from some therapy or counselling that allows them to get in touch with their emotions. Alternatively, something expressive like art therapy, dance therapy or Native American drumming can help them to let their feelings flow. Healing, reiki, shiatsu, acupuncture, aromatherapy or any other alternative treatment that clears blockages might also help.

Semi-simian lines

There are many variations on these, and the situation is similar to the simian line, with perhaps slightly less rigid feelings and behaviour. Sometimes this person is painfully shy, sensitive and introverted. It doesn't look as though either their career or emotional pathways are likely to be easy.

THE FATE LINE

This is my favourite line because it tells so much about the events of a person's life, but it is not an easy one to read. In many ways, it is much easier to 'tell fortunes' by means of the Tarot cards or astrology than by reading hands.

With the Tarot, you can choose the number of cards that you wish to examine, and in astrology, the relevant planets are always sitting there, ready to be analysed. A hand may omit lines, introduce non-standard lines or display lines in every place other than where they should rightly be, and this is frequently the case regarding the fate line. Worse still, there are so many possible scenarios that you will need to look very carefully to see which applies. Reading the fate line needs skill, but it is such an open book to a really great palmist that his clients are often flabbergasted by what he tells them.

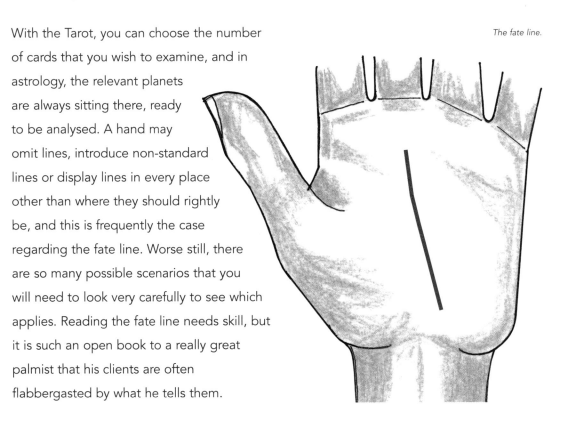

The fate line.

Is there a fate line at all?

If there is a fate line, it will run roughly
upwards, through the
centre of the hand. The
line may start at the
lower end of the hand
and fade out later, or it may
not appear until halfway up
the hand. There may be a
strongly marked fate line that runs
the length of the hand, or there
may be no fate line at all. To be
honest, I am not sure whether it is better
for a person to have a fate line or not –
but it is certainly easier for the palmist if
he does!

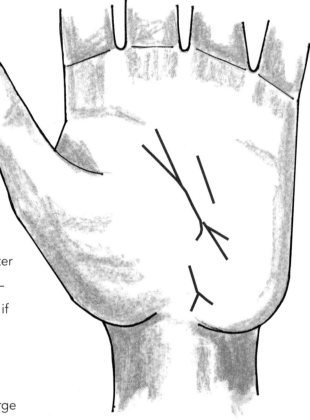

Destiny rules this person's early life.

If there is no fate line whatsoever, the
person is probably more or less in charge
of his own destiny and less likely to suffer
at the whim of fate. If there is a strong fate
line, he will do what fate decrees – whether
or not he enjoys this. A strong, deeply
marked line may indicate an unusual sense
of duty to parents, to a job, to a spouse or family and to making a success of whatever
comes along. At least the fate line indicates
that something will happen during a
person's life.

The start of the fate line

Even the complicated illustration at right doesn't cover all the possibilities because the fate line can rise from the mount of Neptune, the life line, the mount of Venus or the mount of Luna. Here are a few common scenarios and their interpretations.

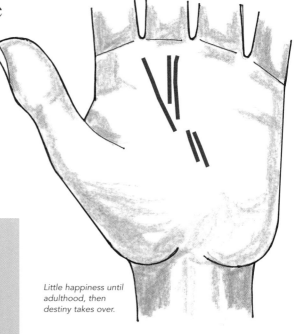

Little happiness until adulthood, then destiny takes over.

- *If the line starts on Neptune, the person will make his decisions during the early part of his life.*

- *When the line starts at the head line, a lucky break may jump-start his career.*

- *If it rises from the life line, or from within the life line on Venus, the person is likely to be influenced (and possibly helped) by his family. He may have been given a good education, a leg-up in business, love, attention, money, esteem and other tangible or non-tangible advantages by them. Alternatively, he may be held back by his family or by an early marriage – or both.*

- *When the line starts on Luna, the family won't have been much help, but outsiders will come to the subject's aid, and he may only really be appreciated by people outside his family. The closer the line is to Venus, the more likely the* person will cling to his family, even as an adult. *His family may dictate to him and he may like it that way or he may simply put up with it.*

- *The closer the line is to Luna, the more likely he is to strike out on his own early on.*

- *If the fate line doesn't start until higher up the hand, the subject has no particular goals during the early stages of his life.*

- *When the line starts at the heart line, it may be love that makes the difference. This also suggests that the subject's later years will be more interesting than the early ones.*

Timing on the fate line

Nothing is cut and dried where timing is concerned, but here is a rough way of working out dates on the fate line.

> • *Take something thin, such as a piece of thread, and run it across the hand from the middle of the knuckle at the base of the thumb and look at the point at which the thread crosses the fate line. This represents the period around the age of 23 to 25.*
> • *The fate line crosses the head line at the age of around 30 to 35.*
> • *The fate line crosses the heart line at around 45 to 50.*
> • *The remaining years are shown in the small area above the heart line.*

The direction of the fate line

The fate line can fade out halfway up the hand, which means that a period of effort has come to an end. Partial fate lines can reappear further up the hand or they may not, indicating a change in fortunes.

Now you must note where the line is heading because if it runs towards Jupiter, the subject will put his heart into a career. If the fate line joins the heart line at the end, he may put his career before his love life. If the fate line heads towards Saturn, the subject will always work hard, which he may, or may not, enjoy, but he will certainly have plenty of work to do. It is unlikely that this line will head towards Apollo, but it can end between Saturn and Apollo, in which case the subject will be happy later in life and be able to spend money on luxuries and pleasures, as well as necessities.

Lines joining the fate line

Probably the most interesting events are those concerning important people who enter the subject's life. These may be friends, lovers, marriage partners, mentors in business, business partners and many others, although the usual scenario is that of love or marriage.

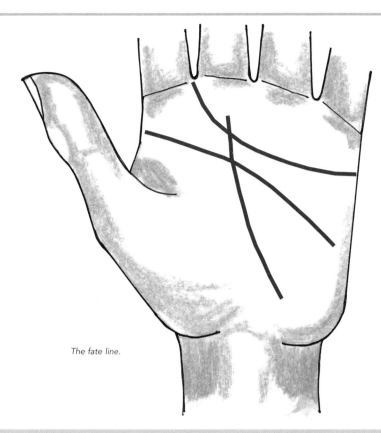

The fate line.

- A relationship will not last if a line joins the fate line for a while and then leaves it again.
- A relationship will last if a line joins the fate line and then becomes part of it.
- The subject chooses his partner from somewhere in his locality. The partner may be a childhood connection, a family friend, a neighbour, a school friend or simply someone from the same area and the same kind of background.
- If this relationship breaks down, the line travels along as part of the fate line for a while and then leaves it on the same side that it entered.
- If it moves through the line and out in the ulna direction, the lover is likely to move on or to move away.
- The lover or person of influence comes from elsewhere when the joining line enters from the ulna side. If the line joins the fate line for a while and then peels off again, see whether the lover remains in the area (towards the radial side) or moves away (towards the ulna side).

Events on the fate line

Any disturbance to the fate line is interesting. An isolated island anywhere on the line suggests a period of confusion, and usually of being short of money. A long island that splits the line in two for part of its route suggests that the person is torn in two directions or trying to cope with two different situations at once.

Bars, breaks, crosses or any other kind of confusion on the line denote setbacks in some area of life. This is most likely to refer to career or financial setbacks, but health problems, divorces or almost anything else could be at the back of the problem; this is where you have to look around the hand for confirmation.

If the fate line doubles, if there are two lines for part of its journey or if a long island has the effect of splitting the line for part of its length, the person's life will be out of phase. He may need to cope with two conflicting demands at the same time, such as holding down a job while caring for young children, or dealing with demanding, elderly parents and a full-time job, or perhaps having to work at two jobs to make ends meet. The subject may feel that he is in the wrong job or living in a way that he doesn't want. If the subject is middle-aged or elderly, he may have regrets and wish that he had done something else with his life.

Moving fate line

Sometimes the fate line breaks and a new line starts above the old, and to the radial or ulna side of the original, often overlapping the original one. In this case, the person changes his life in some important way. If the line overlaps, the chances are that he put the change into action before ending whatever went before. If the new piece of line rises after a slight gap, the change may have been quite sudden, with a new start coming a little later.

The subject will concentrate less on work and more on home life if the new line moves to the ulna side. In this instance, he may change job to be nearer home or he may give up a demanding job for a lighter one. Whatever the reason, he is more interested in home life at that point than work. Sometimes there is no real change, but he spends most of his spare time doing up a home or setting up a family and much

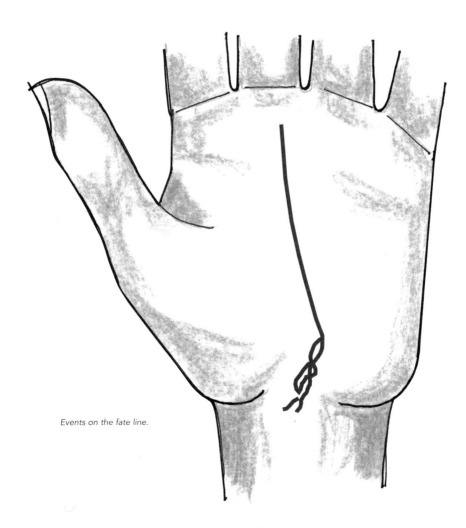

Events on the fate line.

of his time at work thinking about these things. When the line jumps to the radial side, the reverse of all of the above applies, in that the subject becomes more interested in work and less interested in home life.

Sometimes the line breaks up into a number of little lines, and in many cases this is paralleled by small lines forming right across the hand. The person may open a business of his own or take on a job where he has a great variety of tasks to

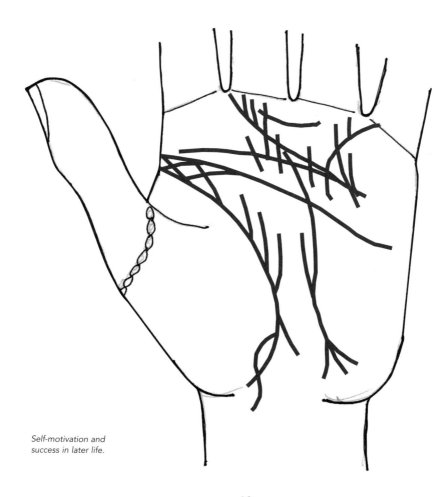

Self-motivation and
success in later life.

cope with. He may put great bursts of energy into something at this point in his life.

A surprisingly common sight is a 'Y'-shaped ending to some part of the fate line. Sometimes this is all that there is, but it is more often followed by a new line that continues its journey. This shows that the subject has become truly fed up with whatever it was that he was doing and that he brought it to an abrupt end. If the new line starts fairly quickly, or even overlaps, he is already on his way to doing something new when this occurs. The technical term for this mark is, 'The boss can take a running jump off a short pier for all I care, I'm off to do something else!" I have heard clients express this in more colourful terms than I have suggested here!

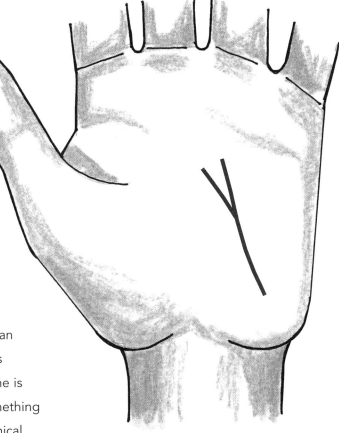

A change of career or lifestyle.

The end of the line.

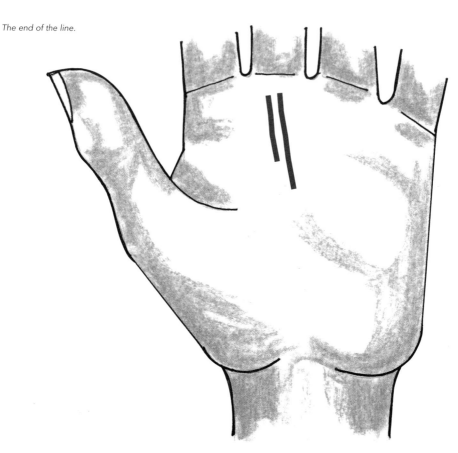

The end of the fate line

- If the line ends on Jupiter, he will achieve personal fulfilment in life, either through a career or perhaps through religious beliefs or some other activity that makes him feel as though it has all been worthwhile.

- The subject can expect to have enough money for fun and pleasure, and probably also a nice home and possibly a good family life later on when the fate line turns towards Apollo at its tail end.

THE APOLLO LINE

This line is sometimes called the sun line, just as the mount and finger of Apollo can also be called the sun mount and finger.

The line of Apollo is concerned with family life, fun, pleasure and creativity. It can signify fame via some creative, artistic or show-business kind of enterprise, or satisfaction from the creation of beauty. If the fate line represents fate and fortune, the Apollo line represents fame and satisfaction from personal (rather than strictly career) achievement. In the lives of ordinary people, it often has something to say about home or property matters.

The Apollo line should be read upwards, moving towards the fingers. This line is often absent, apart from a small section that only travels from the heart line to the

Apollo line.

base of the fingers. When this line is strong and runs up much of the hand, the person may live much of his life in the public eye as a performer, or he may achieve success as an artist or musician. He will certainly be creative, and if this is added to a curved head line, and possibly also a gently percussion edge to the hand, a creative career is definitely indicated.

The start of the Apollo line

If the Apollo line starts very low on the hand and towards the centre of the lower part of the hand, possibly on Neptune, the subject will receive help from his family or from family connections. If a branch enters it from the area of Venus at this lower end, this is even more the case. Often, this line starts on the mount of Luna, which signifies that the person gets his breaks from people and situations outside the home. This also indicates success as a result of using the imagination or intuition. If the Apollo line only appears further up the hand, the person may not be interested in setting up home until later in life, and is less likely to use intuition or a creative imagination for his career, or even as a hobby.

If an early Apollo line is present, the person may set up his own home early in life, or he may get going on a career that he can run from home or a career in an unusual field. Such careers might include artist, writer, fashion designer, make-up artist, master chef, sporting star, dancer, actor, spiritual medium, palmist or anything else that is creative, interesting and personally fulfilling. He may choose quite early on to work from home or to travel around, taking his skills from place to place. Even an electrician, carpenter, builder or plumber can have such a line, especially if he likes his job and uses some creative flair.

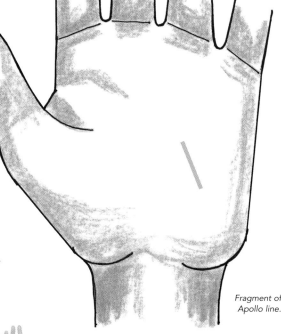

Fragment of
Apollo line.

Events on the line

Many of the same conditions apply to the Apollo line that have already been discussed for the fate line. For example, doubled lines imply a splitting of the person's time and energies, while a break followed by a new line signifies a change of career or a change of address. A line that breaks and jumps towards the ulna side puts the emphasis on home life, while a radial jump takes him out of the home. If the line appears to 'draw' fine lines towards it, the person may start to work from home or to look for a creative outlet.

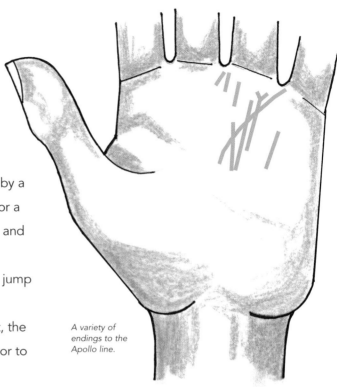

A variety of endings to the Apollo line.

For most people, the Apollo line is less concerned with becoming a Hollywood movie star than with buying, selling, renting, working on and enjoying a property. Use the same information as in the fate line and apply it to property matters – for instance, an island on the line, a bar, a break or any other disturbance will apply to property matters and happiness in family life.

The end of the Apollo line

Frequently, the only part of the Apollo line that actually exists on a hand is the latter part of it, which starts somewhere around the heart line, either just below or above it. This shows happiness in later life, and possibly an ability to turn to sporting, artistic or creative pursuits when the person finally has the leisure and money available for the purpose.

A line that ends by splitting into three splayed branches is called a trident, and this signifies that the person will not be without money, especially later in life. Double-check this by looking at the edge of the hand on the radial (thumb) side for a 'money-maker' line that runs vertically down the side of the mount of Jupiter.

A whole, or a partial, piece of Apollo line at the top of the hands under the fingers suggests domestic security in old age. If this line is close to the mount of Saturn, the subject will live close to his family; if it is closer to the mount of Mercury, he will live closer to his friends or in some place that has a personal attachment for him. If the line ends in a long 'V', he will take care of a parent and

may have the parent living with him for a while.

If it ends in a 'ladder of success', which is a lot of little lines, each one higher on the hand than the last, this is a sign of ultimate success and satisfaction.

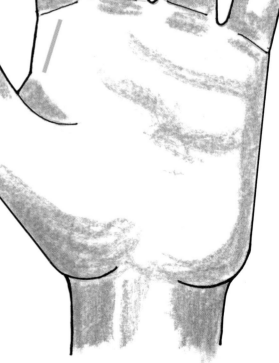

'Money-maker' line.

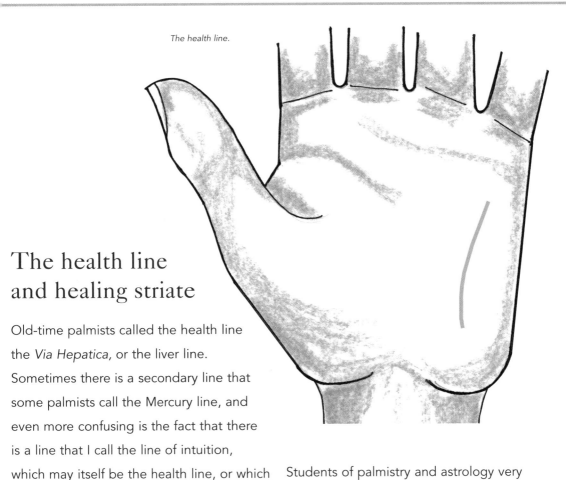

The health line.

The health line and healing striate

Old-time palmists called the health line the *Via Hepatica*, or the liver line. Sometimes there is a secondary line that some palmists call the Mercury line, and even more confusing is the fact that there is a line that I call the line of intuition, which may itself be the health line, or which may be in addition to it. Don't worry too much about the names or which line is which for the moment. Just look at the area of the hand shown in the illustration and see if anything, even the faintest of lines appears, and if there is a line showing, read it upwards from the wrist end.

Students of palmistry and astrology very quickly pick up on the connection between Mercury, the messenger of the gods, and communication, but they tend to miss the fact that Mercury was also the god of a host of other things, including healing, although today's astrologers are also attributing healing to the god Chiron.

The presence of a line or lines in this area suggests that the person is interested in health. If one takes the topics in any magazine or newspaper as a measure of what most people are interested in, health comes high on the list, so finding such a line would hardly be surprising. What is important is whether this is just a generalised interest or a specific one, and why. A chained, broken or islanded health line shows that health is a personal issue. Perhaps the person themselves has health problems, or maybe they have to care for someone else whose health is weak. Take a look at where this line is heading because if it crosses the heart line and enters the mount of Mercury, the interest in health may be more than personal or merely academic. Apart from those who work in the health industry, there are alternative and spiritual healers, and even those who work in hair and beauty salons or the diet industry. In some cases, the person will work in the fields of psychiatry, psychology, counselling, astrology, palmistry or channelling.

If there is a line that curves around the percussion side of the hand, regardless of whether it ends up on Mercury or not, the subject will be extremely intuitive, and probably psychic.

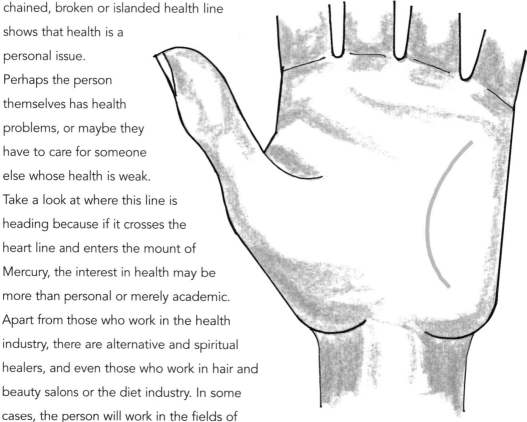

This indicates intuition and psychic gifts.

Sometimes the line appears to be almost as strong as one of the other lines on the hand, certainly as strong as a fate or Apollo line. If this is the case, or if your eye is drawn to redness in this area at the time of the reading, there is likely to be something on the subject's mind. If the health or any line in this area of the hand travels up and touches one of the attachment lines, this suggests that a love affair, passion or obsession is upsetting the subject.

Healing striate

You sometimes see healing striate spelled as healing striata. The spelling is not right, but it isn't a surprising mistake to make because that is how the word is pronounced. It comes from the same root as the word 'striation'.

Sometimes the health line runs into the striate. This means that health and healing are important to the subject, and he may well work in the health field in some guise, including in such things as spiritual healing or even working as a vet. There are very few really clear-cut marks on the hand, but this is one that palmists always take into account. The healing striate is composed of three parallel lines, which lie on a slight diagonal on the mount of Mercury, and they are frequently crossed by another line that runs diagonally through them. Even without a health line running into these, the subject will have the gift of healing bodies and minds.

Love and relationship lines

Always look at both hands for evidence about the lines that you will see in this section because the minor hand can actually be more revealing or accurate when dealing with this emotive area of a person's life.

The attachment lines are little creases that enter the palm horizontally from the percussion edge of the hand in the area between the bottom of the little finger and the heart line. There is some confusion because some old-time palmistry books say that these lines show the number of children that a person will have, but this is not so.

I will talk here about partnerships, relationships and even marriage, but these lines simply refer to those who we have especially strong feelings about. The system works in the same way for gay lovers as for straight ones. These lines sometimes even refer to very strong friendships or even

flatmates, but the usually interpretation is that of relationships that include strong feelings, love, sex, affairs or living together in any form of 'marriage'.

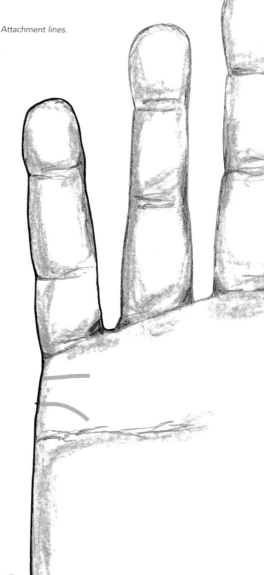

Attachment lines.

The number of lines

There may be one strong line, two lines, more than two or a number of vague lines, with perhaps a few vague ones surrounding one line that is somewhat stronger. These lines appear, disappear and change their appearance remarkably rapidly. Marriage certificates are important in legal terms, but the hand talks about feelings rather than paperwork. In some cases, an actual marriage may leave only a faint or stunted line, while an affair can leave a disproportionately heavy one.

Right from the start, we find ourselves in the murky area of potential and reality. It would be nice to say that one line means one attachment, two means two and so on, but this area of hand-reading is all about needs, feelings and what goes on in a person's head rather than concrete facts, or even what we would like the outside world to see. You will see what I mean as we go through this section.

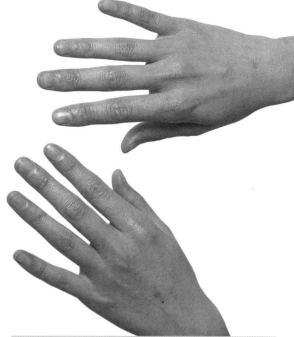

- *Although there is no hard and fast rule, I have found that it works well if you read these lines by starting with the lowest and working upwards.*
- *Always read both hands and remember that the minor hand often shows the true emotional picture.*

One strong attachment line can mean one long partnership, but it can also show what the subject wants in an ideal world. If a relationship fails, this person will try to find another, and then tries to make that one work. The subject is romantic rather than calculating, loving and giving rather than cautious and self-preserving. He (or, more likely, she) buys into the romantic business of finding a soul mate or falling into the arms of a lover who understands him or who supplies him with every emotional requirement. If this person is lucky, the first time around this may end up as a true romance.

If such a subject has more than one relationship during his lifetime, he will probably only be able to concentrate on one at a time. If there is an affair during marriage, it may be that the affair is what counts in emotional terms. In short, the person has one deep and abiding love during the course of his life, and anything else pales into insignificance. If you are faced with someone who has had – and lost – a lover of this ilk, don't make them feel that their emotional life is over, but simply tell them that they will never forget this person, but that they can love again. In many cases, an additional line will grow above the original one later on.

When there are two lines, the subject considers what he is getting out of the relationship rather than simply trying to make the best of it. He will question whether he really wants to stay in a particular partnership forever. He may not admit this to other members of his family, or even to his friends, but somewhere in his head the small voice of logic tells him that all is not perhaps as it should be. Two marriages are a strong possibility for this subject.

Concerning the relationship

There are many factors to look at here, and some are not pleasant. I will now give you an example of what I mean by starting with the worst-case scenario – that of foretelling the death of a partner.

If the attachment line becomes deeper, slightly chained and turns up to touch the crease at the base of the Mercury finger, or if there is a separate ring under the Mercury finger, the person will lose a partner through death. This mark seems to form on the hands a few years before the death occurs.

I had this mark on my hand, which meant that I had the horrible knowledge that my then husband, Tony Fenton, must have had something terminally wrong with him. He died a few years after I first noticed the mark. I have since remarried and the mark has now gone.

Before leaving the subject of unpleasant marks on a hand, if a person takes a decision to change a difficult situation, the lines can change. Even something as difficult as a widow line can vanish if steps are taken to improve the partner's health. Please use great caution when giving this kind of information to a client, as even I, with all of my insight, spiritual strength, knowledge of divination and psychology, found the information sitting on my own hand very difficult to cope with.

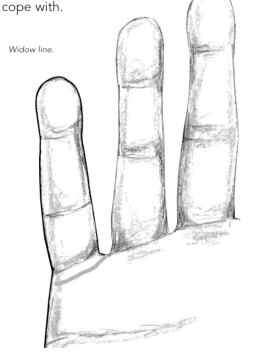

Widow line.

Here are some other good and bad events to be seen on the attachment lines.

- An island on an attachment line (b) suggests that the partner is sick or is likely to become sick. Alternatively, the partner may have financial or business problems on his mind.

- A forked line or a frayed line (a) suggests that the relationship is in difficulties.

- Parallel lines (c) suggest that the partners coexist, but that the marriage is not emotionally satisfying.

- A line that is doubled at the percussion edge, but that blends into one line, shows a strong element of friendship in the marriage, and it is possible that the partners started out as friends before getting together.

- A line that has a finer companion line above or beneath suggests that the person has other interests apart from the partner. There may be any of a thousand other things that come between the subject and complete concentration on his partner, but an affair outside marriage is a fair bet.

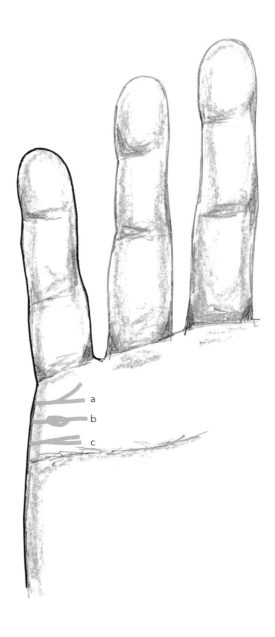

Another personal story – this time, a funny one!

About 15 years ago, I took one of those training courses given by the Local Education Authority, which gave me a certificate that allowed me to teach in adult education anywhere in the world. Towards the end of the course, we all had to do a set piece using materials and methods of our choice. I chose to give a talk on palmistry using an overhead projector. The head of the college and other luminaries were present for the event, which took place in the college's lecture theatre. The vice president of the college had agreed to be the guinea pig for this. While interpreting the lines on the print, I casually mentioned the companion line, and, before I could stop myself, I told the audience that this man was clearly involved in both a marriage and a long-standing affair. He agreed that this was the case!

If a deletion line appears close to, or running through, this line, the marriage is on the rocks and a split is likely.

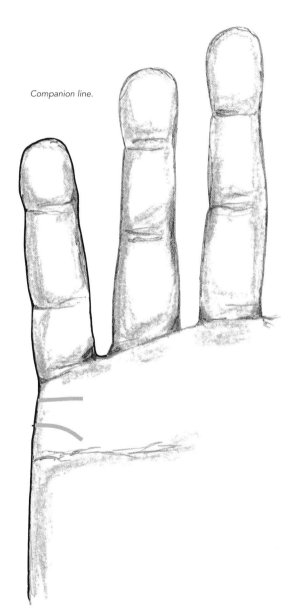

Companion line.

- When the line curves downwards, the marriage is disappointing and the person will be put upon. A divorce is likely at some point, and if a deletion line crosses the attachment line, the chances are that it is well on the way.

- A small fork signals a sudden end to the marriage. In the words of a friend who had put up with a violent husband for many years, 'One day, a bell went in my head and I thought that this couldn't go on any longer – a week later, I walked out.'

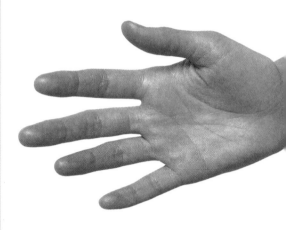

An attachment line that rises upwards says that the partner is doing well in his or her career. If a little line rises from somewhere along this line, the partner may not start out a success, but he or she will become so later on. If a line falls from the attachment line, the partner could lose a job, money or status.

Sometimes a few lines run across the hands and cross or touch other lines. These denote outside interference in the person's life. If they touch the head line, they can interfere in his choice of education or in the way that he runs his working life. If they touch or cross the heart line or attachment lines, family members, in-laws or others interfere in the person's private life, and this can even go so far as to wreck a marriage.

A final word

One or two nice, clear lines show that the subject is likely to have only one or two deep relationships during his life, but that they should be happy ones.

Travel lines

Before we look at the subject of travel in detail, let us clear up one old wives' tale about the so-called *Via Lasciva*.

Very old books call this line the *Via Lasciva* and they tell us that the line shows a lascivious nature or perverted sexuality. Other old books called this the 'poison line' because the person who has this line is said to be in danger of becoming a victim of poisoning. Both ideas are extremely dramatic, and while I can't agree with the idea of a person with this line being lascivious, I can see where the poison idea comes from. Modern palmists call this the 'allergy line' because they have discovered that those who have this line suffer from allergies. Those with a *Via Lasciva* do

seem to be sensitive to drugs, food and chemicals, and many have asthma, hay fever, migraine or eczema.

Another common feature of this line that is totally unrelated to allergies is the connection to foreign countries and peoples. Many people who have this line

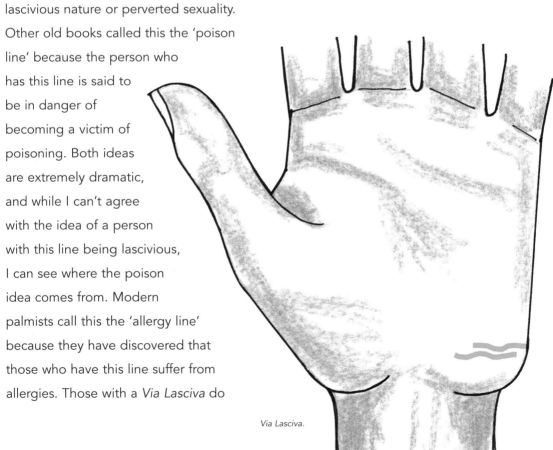

Via Lasciva.

have friends or relatives who live in far-distant countries, and they probably have to 'cross water', as the Gypsies used to say, in order to see them. If this line touches, or throws a branch to, the life line, it often means that the subject will spend time away from his own country, and that he may even emigrate.

Other travel lines

Travel lines appear on the percussion side of the hand, all the way down from the heart line to the bottom of the hand. There may be a few or many, some may be strong and others weak, or there may be many faint lines.

The stronger the line, the more important an individual country, or perhaps an individual trip, is, while many faint lines might belong to someone who travels a great deal. This subject can't be cut and dried because hands vary so much, but the system works far better than one would expect. In some cases, the connection may

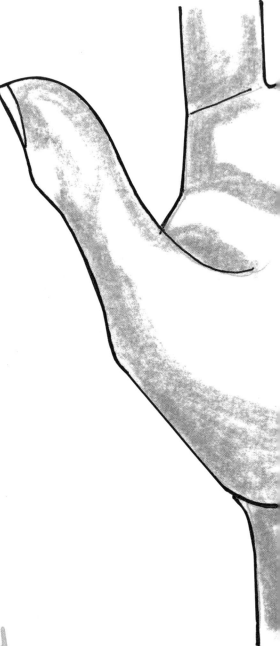

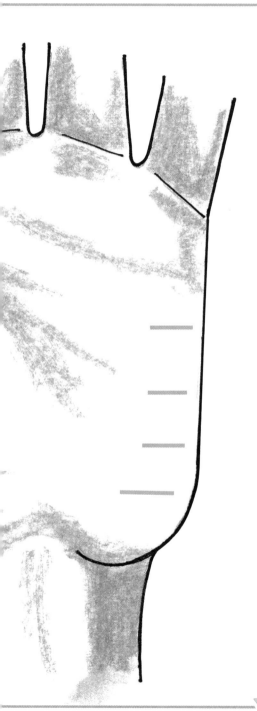

simply be a business one, and the person doesn't actually travel to the countries at all.

The following list applies to everybody, wherever they happen to have been born.

- Between the heart and head line: Scandinavia and Europe.
- Around the end of the head line: the Mediterranean, Eastern Europe and the Middle East.
- Long, straight lines on Mars/Luna: USA, Canada, Caribbean, South America and Russia.
- Mid-Luna: India, Pakistan, Sri Lanka, Seychelles and other Gulf States and Asian countries.
- Lower Luna: China, Korea, Japan.
- Pluto: Australia, South Africa, New Zealand.

Disturbances on the travel lines

- Island: a problem trip, possibly due to illness while travelling.
- Break: a broken journey.
- Double: two journeys in quick succession.
- Disturbed or frayed: a bothersome trip or a wasted journey.

OTHER LINES

Child lines

Child lines run vertically through the attachment lines. These are notoriously difficult for even a good palmist to deal with, and they are often very fine and difficult to see. Try sprinkling a little talcum powder on this area of the hand because that helps such fine lines to show up more clearly. These lines are usually on the edge of the palm, where it begins to curve into the percussion side of the hand. The line should cut through at least one of the attachment lines.

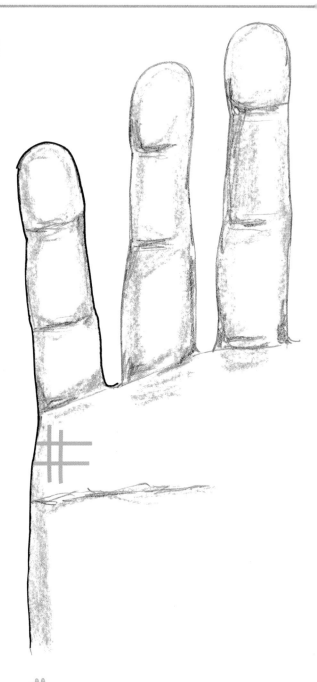

Child lines (sons).

Generally speaking, one line means one child, two means two children and so on. Straight lines tend to refer to sons, while sloping ones tend to refer to daughters. However, this can refer to the type of child, as a gentle, artistic boy sometimes shows up as a sloping line and vice versa. When child lines are close together, the children will be close in age. A gap may show that the children are dissimilar to each other or simply that there is a gap in their ages. A person who looks after children, or who teaches them, and who enjoys doing so, may have many fine lines here. The same goes for those who own or care for animals.

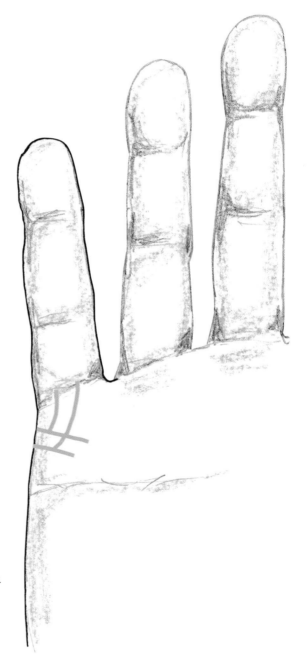

Child lines (daughters).

Disturbances on the line

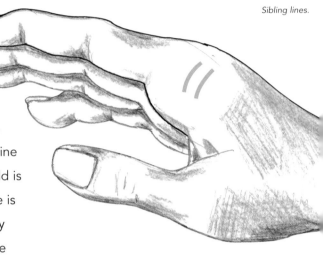

Sibling lines.

The rules for disturbances on the child lines are similar to those for any other line. In short, if the line is disturbed, there is a problem. A child line with an island on it suggests that a child is sick or troubled in some way. If the line is split, has a deletion line across it or any other disturbance, it is worth asking the subject what (if anything) is wrong either with the child or between the parents and the child. Lines that fizzle out, with or without an island, or lines that wriggle and wander, but don't go far enough to cut through an attachment line, can indicate miscarriages or abortions. Sometimes a perfectly normal line can indicate a child who never made it into life for some reason.

Sibling lines

Sibling lines are found on the opposite side of the hand to attachment lines, and they refer to brothers and sisters.

These can be read in more or less the same way as attachment lines because such marks as islands, stars on the lines or a break in the line suggest that a brother or sister has a problem. The classic problem mark is a patch of redness in this area. It would be nice to be able to say that one sibling line denotes one brother or sister, two signify two and so on, but this doesn't always work. Once again, the lines probably say more about the way one feels about siblings than the reality of who is related to whom. Cousins, and even childhood neighbours and friends, can show up here if they were (or still are) important to the subject.

Rings and girdles

The ring of Solomon, which is found on the mount of Jupiter, belongs to someone with wisdom who can listen to others and give good advice. It is common to see this on the hands of counsellors, advisors, bank managers, solicitors, social workers and others who help the public.

Rings that run around under one of the fingers are rare, and they suggest something unusual in the personality. A secondary crease under Jupiter suggests that something is cramping the subject's ego. A crease under Saturn suggests that the subject is a real misery and a loner. A ring of Mercury or an extra crease under the little finger can indicate the death of a partner, difficulties in business or great success, but difficulties in relationships.

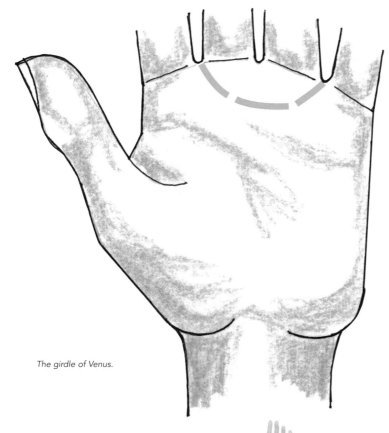

The girdle of Venus.

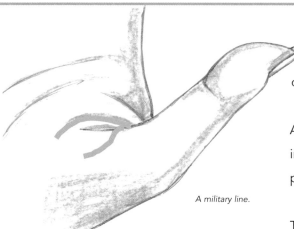

A military line.

is to understand the mount that they appear on or the line that they appear close to. Here are a few examples.

A short line running down lower Mars indicates a scout master, paramilitary person or youth leader.

The crease that is formed where the thumb joins the mount of Venus is called the family line, but this is a misnomer because it really relates to the home, or homes, that a person may have. More than one line here suggests more than one home, possibly at the same time. Such a person may have a holiday home, a time-share or some other property or premises. The more settled the person's life is, the more settled this line will be, but if he moves around a lot, the line will be disturbed or disjointed. If you want to follow up my theory about homes, land, goods and chattels, also look for vertical lines on Venus.

The most common of the rings and girdles is the girdle of Venus, which occurs beneath the two middle fingers. Sometimes this girdle is complete, but often it is broken or only parts of it appear. Either way, the girdle of Venus belongs to a sensitive person who may also be intuitive or psychic. A partial girdle is nice because it shows an ability to make friends easily, but a whole one does seem to suggest that the person is self-absorbed, self-protective, self-motivated, self-centred and possibly just plain selfish.

Other minor lines

There are dozens of stray lines that appear on a hand, and the best way to read them

Two small lines that run into the junction of the Apollo and Mercury fingers denote an interest in spiritual matters and the chance of another incarnation to come.

A fine line running down the radial side of the mount of Jupiter, almost at the side of the hand, is a money-maker line.

Many hands display a kind of crease that is formed later in life by the way that the thumb folds. This crease starts from somewhere on the crease at the base of the thumb, crosses the mount of Venus and then goes on out into the hand. If this runs upwards, the person habitually looks back to the past, while if it runs downwards, they look forward to the future.

Curve of intuition

It is common to see this line on the hands of psychics or those who are deeply interested in psychic and intuitive matters. This can be confusing because it can take the place of the health line, or it can appear next to the health line. If it is alone, the subject is more likely to be interested in divination, palmistry and mental health. If it accompanies a health line, the subject is also interested in health and healing.

These are the main minor lines, but there are many more stray lines that turn up on hands, and the best way to approach them is to understand the meaning of each mount and also to see whether the line is clear or disturbed. For instance, a disturbed line on Luna suggests that a creative or imaginative project goes wrong for some reason, while a clear line in Jupiter indicates the achievement of an objective.

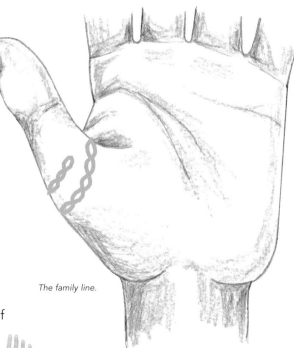

The family line.

Marks

Old-time palmistry books harp on about certain

marks and designs on a hand, and they sometimes

give really dire warnings about their meanings.

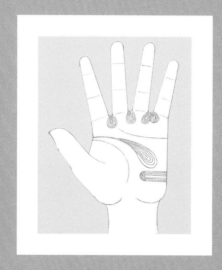

MARKS

To my mind, many marks come and go, and most just emphasise a situation that is ongoing at the time of the reading. For this reason, Asian palmists and some Gypsy and clairvoyant palmists concentrate more on these marks than we do in the West.

They use them to open the doors of their intuition because the marks alert them to a particular event shown by the shape of the mark or discolouration. This system is similar to the way that some clairvoyants read tea leaves or coffee grounds. The following are the most common marks.

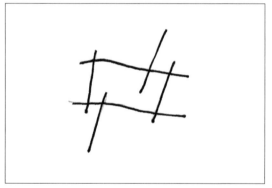

The square.

The square

The square is often seen on the mount of Jupiter, where it seems to act as a form of protection to the person. This subject will overcome setbacks and rise again after setbacks. An isolated square on a line is being restricted in some way. This would mean a poor, or non-existent, love life if on the heart line; educational or career problems if on the head line; and general problems if on the life line.

The cross

Old-timers hated crosses and stars, saying that these brought dreadful luck. According to some old books, a cross on Luna meant death by drowning, and a cross on Saturn meant death on the gallows. This is rubbish! In my experience, a cross on Luna seems to indicate an important voyage on, or over, water – but one from which the subject definitely returns in one piece. Crosses on Apollo seem to mean winning a lottery or raffle or money that comes in long after the work has been done, as is the case with royalties. Incidentally, check for a line being thrown from the fate line towards the mount of Mercury for success as a writer. A star that has a red colour often does indicate some kind of problem, especially if this is on an attachment, child or sibling line.

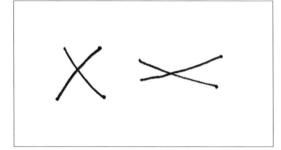

The cross.

Other marks

Here are a few more marks.

- Triangle: talent.
- Diamond: feelings of imprisonment.
- Stray lines: interference.
- Tassel: vitamin deficiency or worry.
- Grille: sickness. A grille is a mark that looks like the mesh pattern of a sieve or a tennis racquet, and this always indicates illness. The grille goes when the person recovers.
- Dots: dots, or tiny pits, on a line, or, indeed, anywhere on the hand, are important because they indicate illness. When my first husband developed a kidney stone, a deep pit suddenly appeared on his health line. When the stone 'passed', the dot went away.

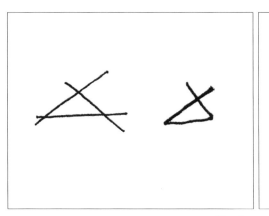

Triangles.

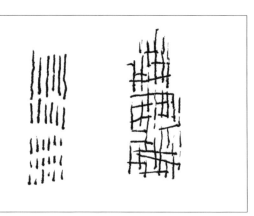

The girdle.

I have read comments about circles in old books, and these were always considered to be indications of doom and gloom – but in all my years, I have never seen an isolated circle on a hand.

Finally, if you see a mark that looks like something that you recognise, such as a fish, a car, a rocket, an engagement ring, a bouquet, a wedding bell, skis, an aeroplane or anything else that strikes your fancy, mention this to your subject and see what they have to say about it. Such a mark might contain a message about the future.

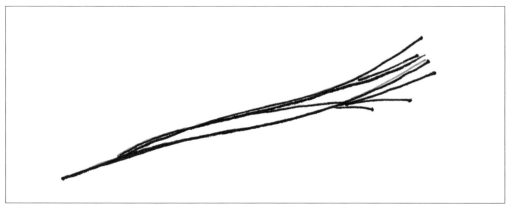

Tassels.

Skin-ridge patterns.

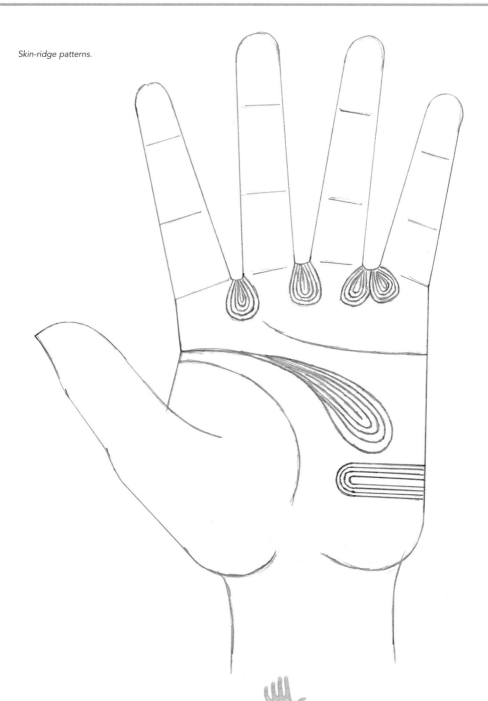

Skin-ridge patterns

We are familiar with the idea of skin-ridge patterns from all of those police programmes on television where the police take, or study, fingerprints, but there are skin-ridge patterns all over the hand. The main thing to bear in mind is that unlike the lines on a hand, the skin-ridge patterns don't change their position, although they can change their appearance due to age and health issues.

Skin-ridge patterns are formed at around eight to nine weeks of gestation, and they stay with us throughout life. There are people who share the same pattern as others on one or two fingers, and there are cases where the police have mistaken the identity of a person due to this. However, nobody has the same pattern throughout the whole hand – not even twins. The fact that these patterns are unchanging means that fingerprints held on police or armed-service files can be referred to years later.

- *Between the Apollo and Mercury fingers: the loop of humour. This shows a sense of humour and often also a love of animals. A whorl in the same area as the loop of humour definitely means an animal lover.*
- *Between the Apollo and Mercury fingers: the loop of style. This shows dress sense and an eye for colour and décor. This can also indicate vanity. Some people have both a loop of humour and a loop of style.*
- *Between the Saturn and Apollo fingers: the loop of serious intent. This gives the subject a capacity for hard work. This person probably works hard throughout life, but he can make a success of himself as a result.*
- *Below the head line: the memory loop. This denotes a good memory for names, dates etc.*
- *On the ulna: the ulna loop. This signifies a love of the countryside and of nature.*
- *Between the Jupiter and Apollo fingers: the rajah loop. This means that the person has royal blood running through his veins. The royalty may be Asian, European or anything else, but if the loop is there, the blue blood is also there.*

Changes in skin-ridge patterns occur through wear and tear, but if the person takes a break from whatever work caused the wear, the skin repairs itself. Patterns become muddied on the fingertips when we get old, and they may almost be obliterated in the case of partially sighted or blind people, or those who lose their sight in old age. Alcoholism and drug addiction will make the long ridges break up into 'strings of pearls', or something that looks like the crenellations on a castle (especially those on Luna).

Apart from the fingerprints, some people have loops, and sometimes even whorls, on various areas of the hands, and the previous page gives a list of the more common ones.

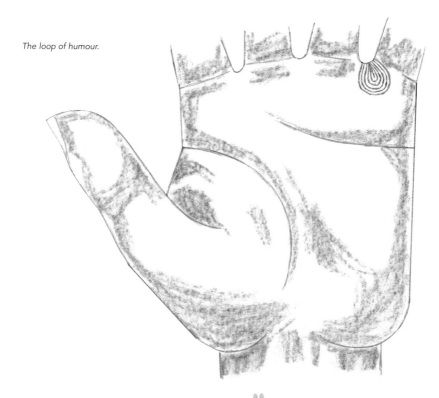

The loop of humour.

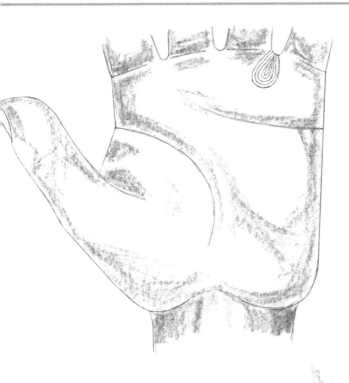

The loop of style.

The loop of memory.

I remember some years ago, when working at a big festival, I saw a couple of Asian people with rajah loops and mentioned to them that they were supposedly related to Indian or Pakistani royalty. They admitted that they came from upper-class families and that this was entirely possible. Later that week, I read for two white men who had slight Continental accents. They were brothers and both had rajah loops on both their major and minor hands. I pointed out that it was rare for someone to have a rajah loop on one hand, but having them on both hands was extremely unusual, and it was even more odd for both brothers to have this mark. I said that they must belong to one of the old European royal families. They were amazed, and then told me that they were dukes of Braganza, which was once the Portuguese royal family!

The loop of serious intent.

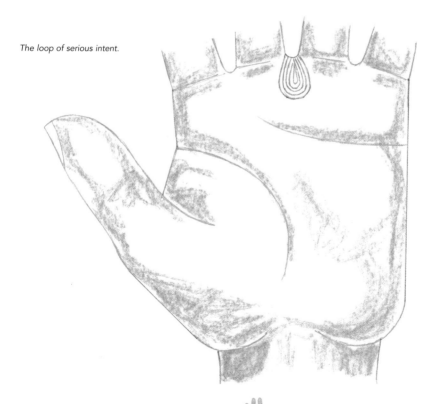

The rajah loop.

The Ulna loop.

Health on
the hands

This is such a vast subject that it would easily fill a

book by itself, but this chapter provides an overview

of how health issues can be signposted on the hands.

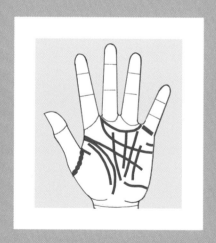

HEALTH ON THE HANDS

In this chapter, we will touch on some obvious health matters and leave the denser medical histories for those who study hand-reading specifically for this purpose.

First, consider which hand you are looking at because the minor hand shows health problems that are building up even before the person is aware of them, but it can also show past problems. The major hand shows the current situation.

Older readers may actually have been to doctors who looked at hands to check certain health matters, but unfortunately this aspect of medical diagnosis is rarely used these days. Doctors regularly used to check for anaemia by pressing down on a nail, then taking their hand away and seeing how long it took for the blood to return. They also checked for psoriasis and other disorders from the nails.

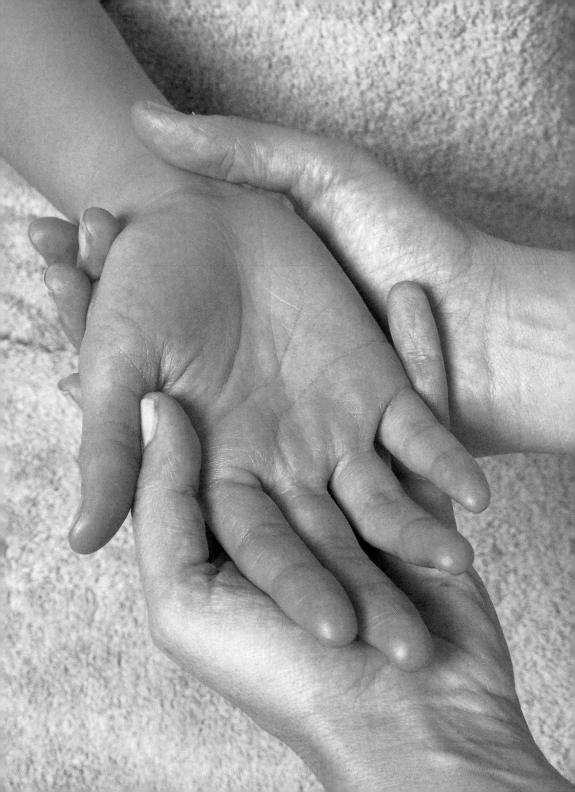

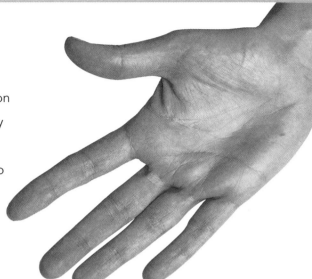

General appearance

Soft hands belong to those who want an easy life, but they can also be an indication of sickness or thyroid problems, especially if the skin feels like cellophane stretched over some kind of gel filling. Softness also occurs during pregnancy and in the hands of vegetarians.

Temperature

- *Hot, sweaty hands signify possible thyroid or glandular disorders.*
- *Hot, dry hands can indicate blood-pressure or kidney disorders and fever.*
- *Cold hands indicate poor circulation, shock or fever.*
- *Clammy hands denote a sluggish liver.*
- *Cold patches suggest uneven circulation due to heart disorders, especially when different parts of the fingers are cooler than others.*

Colour

- *Red: a smoker.*
- *Pale: poor circulation or anaemia.*
- *Grey/lilac/bluish: heart trouble.*
- *Yellow: liver trouble.*

Redness on the percussion may indicate blood-pressure or glandular problems. On Luna or upper Mars, this may indicate diabetes or kidney disorders.

Rascettes

The bracelets at the wrist, or rascettes, as palmists call them, should be straight.

Tradition says that there should be three rascettes for a long life, with each rascette representing thirty years of life.

This is not worth using as a hard and fast rule, but it is worth worrying if the upper rascette breaks up and reaches into the palm as this may indicate heart or lung problems.

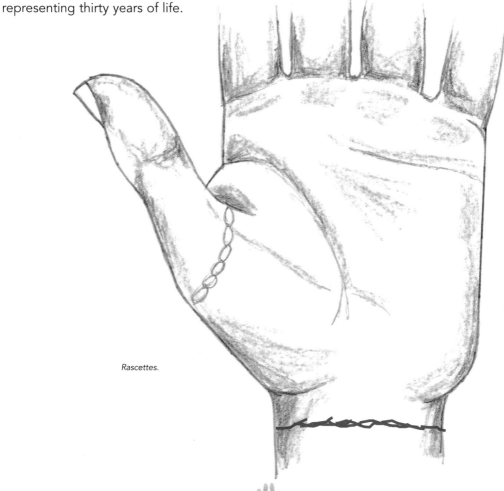

Rascettes.

The major lines

Pits along the life line indicate spinal problems. The neck is represented at the start of the line and the tail, at the end. Breaks can indicate accidents and illnesses or emotional shocks to the system.

Chains on the head line indicate headaches or migraine. Islands on this or the heart line can indicate dental, sight or hearing problems. A break might indicate a head injury. A truly strange head line with huge islands is a sign of mental illness. A strange formation on the percussion that looks like a pair of tongs grabbing the end of the head line indicates insomnia.

Flakiness at the start of the heart line under the Mercury mount is a sign of heart

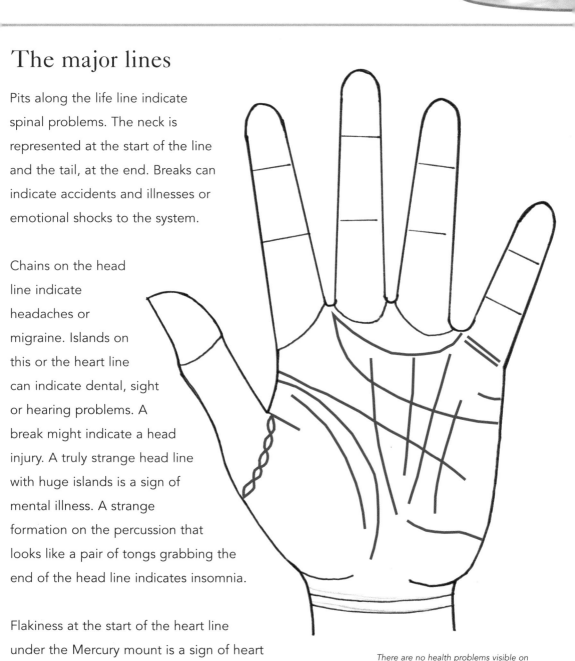

There are no health problems visible on this lucky hand.

trouble. Any disturbance or island under Saturn/Jupiter, where the line starts to bend upwards, is an indication of breast problems. Feathering along the line can mean a shortage of potassium. If the person suffers from depression, suggest that he takes potassium as this will make a great improvement to his life.

A raised area in the skin-ridge pattern just above the heart line that points towards the place where the Apollo and Mercury fingers join can indicate heart trouble. Another indication is seen when the area

around the heart line under Mercury or Apollo is hard to the touch.

Dots, pits, blue marks or anything else that is strange on any line can mean inflammation in some area of the body.

An assortment of health indicators

Disturbances low down on the mount of Neptune indicate problems for women. If there is a triangle formation there that suddenly fills up with fine, broken bits of

Healthy nails.

Rheumatism, arthritis or old age.

Tuberculosis or lung cancer.

Lateral dents.

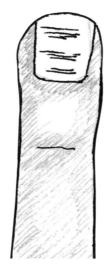

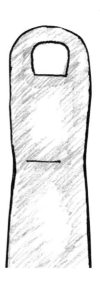

Tiny nails.

line or that becomes red, pregnancy is the answer!

A single wart represents a psychological blockage. If this is on the palm side of the hand, the person is causing the blockage himself and you can easily see which area of life is being blocked by checking out the appropriate mount, finger or line. If it is on the back of the hand, the problem is being caused by someone else. Once again, relate this to the part of the hand or the finger in question. Redness on the back of any finger shows a temporary problem in that area of life. This is caused by someone other than the subject himself. Many warts, or warts on a child's hands, are meaningless.

Fingernails take around six to eight months to grow out from root to tip, so they show current or recent health and emotional problems.

- *Lateral dents: an ailment, the flu, a virus, a shock or weight loss during the previous six to eight months.*
- *Longitudinal ridges: trouble with the bones and surrounding ligaments. If the ridge is on the thumb or Jupiter finger, the problem is in, or near, the head. When on the Saturn finger, the shoulders, spine, ribs or pelvis may have been broken. On the Apollo finger, the arms and legs will have been hurt, and if on the Mercury finger, the forearms, wrists, lower legs, ankles and feet may be damaged.*
- *Watchglass or Hippocratic nails: tuberculosis or lung cancer. Slightly turned-under nails also indicate lung problems.*
- *Spoon-shaped nails: nutritional deficiencies or brain damage.*
- *Pits on nails: psoriasis. Ditto an overgrowth of skin around the nails.*
- *White spots: shortage of vitamin A and D, calcium and zinc.*
- *Dark patches: fungal infection in the stomach and sexual organs.*
- *Tunnel nails: spinal problems.*
- *Yellow nails: jaundice, liver damage.*
- *Brown nails or half the nail one colour and half another colour: kidney problems.*
- *Tiny nails: stomach problem.*

Nutritional deficiency or brain damage.

Other features

Lines running across the fingertips come and go as changes occur in a person's hormone levels, especially when the oestrogen is running down. Middle-aged women's hands improve if they take HRT or some alternative remedy that helps to regulate this.

Some older palmistry books say that large moons on a hand indicate heart problems or a potential for strokes. I have not found this to be the case, but if the moons suddenly change shape or become larger or smaller than usual, this can be so. Also, if the nails are blue/grey/mauve in colour, there will be such problems. Palpitations can make the nails temporarily bluish, but they return to their normal pink colour when the palpitations stop.

Grilles denote severe shock or trauma to the part of the body that the area of the hand represents, e.g., heart, head, spine, centre of the body or reproductive organs. Grilles are hard to recognise as they may not look like netting as much as smudgy areas. Small, glassy warts on the radial edge of the hand below the thumb, or

around the attachment lines, indicate tumours that may (or may not) be due to cancer. Hands that look old, despite the fact that the person is not particularly old, signify asthma or allergies.

Some medicines cause changes in the appearance of the hands; when the person stops taking these, their hands should return to normal.

The main thing is not to become paranoid about your health because the chances are that you are reading more into this than is necessary.

Grilles or other disturbances.

Tunnel.

Taking handprints

TAKING HANDPRINTS

A quick way to make a handprint is to cover the hand with dark lipstick and then place the hand onto some fine or flimsy paper, pressing the paper gently up, into the centre of the hand, and then peeling it off. However, if you are going to do the job properly, you will need the right tools.

You will need this equipment.

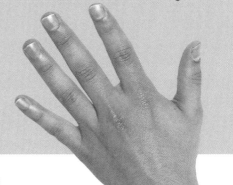

- Paint or ink – water-based, and in a tube that looks like a small, old-fashioned tube of toothpaste. The consistency is much the same as toothpaste. The ink comes in many colours, so you can experiment as you wish. Oil-based inks smear, and they are hard to wash off the hands or clothes if they get on to them. It is possible to buy fingerprint ink from art shops. This is much finer-grained than the other kind, but it is oil-based and really difficult to use for whole hands – and it is very messy.
- Roller – a rubber-coated paste-up roller, about 5cm/2in wide and 2.5cm/1in in diameter.
- A tile or plate – the kind of tile that is used for kitchen and bathroom walls is ideal, otherwise use an old, large plate that you no longer need.

- Kitchen paper.
- Pen – felt-tipped for drawing around the hand.
- Paper – normal photocopy paper will do: this job doesn't require anything special, and really good papers will probably do a worse job than inexpensive ones.
- Also . . . aprons or old clothes, access to soap and water and old towels for cleaning.

Method

1 Put several sheets of kitchen paper on top of each other to make a soft base. Take a couple more sheets and fold them in half in order to make a slight ridge or mound. Lay several sheets of photocopy paper on the top. Squeeze a little of the ink on to your plate or tile, about 1.5cm/½in will do. Run the roller up and down in the ink until it is well covered, but not too thick or wet. Now hold the hand out nice and straight and cover it with the ink. Don't put on too much ink or the print will smudge.

2 Relax the hand a little, then place it on the paper, with the palm positioned over the slight mound in the middle. Then press lightly over the area where the fingers and thumb join the hand. Leave the hand in place for a moment or two and then take the felt-tipped pen and draw round it. Don't angle the pen in, around the fingers, or you will spoil their shape. If you can't get between two fingers, don't push the pen in, just go around the tops. Now hold the paper down at the top and bottom and slowly lift the hand, beginning from the wrist.

3 Record whether this was the left or right hand, and if you are compiling a file of handprints, always include the person's name and age and the print date. Do the same with the other hand and leave the prints to dry completely. Once dry, photocopy the print if possible and put the original into a plastic pocket for safe-keeping.

4 If the hand is hollow in the middle, you will end up with a gap. In this case, take another print and go as far as outlining the hand with the felt-tipped pen. Then carefully lift the hand up a little at the wrist end, with the paper still stuck to it, and slowly and gently reach under the third sheet below the hand and gently press your fingers into the middle of the palm. It is worth noting that money comes to those who have a slight hollow in their hands – although they usually have to earn it the hard way! If you still can't get a reasonable print of the centre of the hand,

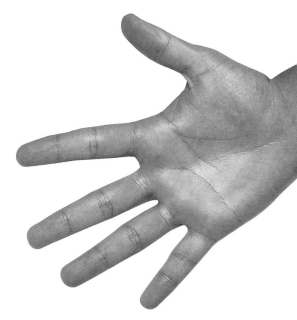

rest the bottom of a piece of paper on a rolling pin or a wine bottle and put the heel of the hand on this. Roll the pin forwards and allow the hand to rest on the paper as it rolls along. This will distort the finger shapes, but it will give you a print of the middle of the hand. In this case, pin your two types of print together so that you have all the information for your files.

PSYCHIC DEVELOPMENT

If you are keen to develop your psychic powers, the best approach is to join a group or organisation that specialises in teaching this, and your choice of approach will depend upon your own outlook and preferences.

Perhaps you would like to join a development circle at your spiritualist church, or you may decide that witchcraft is your route. You may already know that you have a certain amount of ESP, or perhaps you have developed this for yourself by reading the Tarot or by using psychometry (the art of holding a piece of jewellery or some other object in order to tune into a person). If so, you can always start by reading a hand scientifically and then allow any impressions to come into your mind later on.

A good trick is to peer at a hand with your eyes slightly out of focus, as though you were staring into space. Allow the marks and lines in the centre of the hand to run into each other and to form patterns, then, if anything then comes to mind, pass on your message and see what happens. It is even possible to use the marks, blotches, lines and patterns that appear in the centre of a hand in the same way that a tea-leaf-reader or coffee-ground-reader might do by interpreting the meanings of the shapes that are formed. An example would be of a mark that suddenly began to take the shape of an envelope, meaning that an important message is on the way – or perhaps a dagger, indicating enemies or treachery at hand, or perhaps a bee, which would suggest busy times ahead.

So the choice is yours, because you can read hands scientifically at all times or use a mixture of intuition and science. You may find one person easy to tune into psychically and the next person difficult, in which case if you have a sound basis in scientific palmistry, you can still read for them. You may use pure psychometry, or you can use my 'tea-leaf' method, or you can use any, or all, of the above on some occasions and not on others. At the end of the day, if you know how to read hands scientifically, you can read from handprints or even descriptions of a hand. If you will pardon the pun, this is a 'handy' skill to have – even for a clairvoyant.

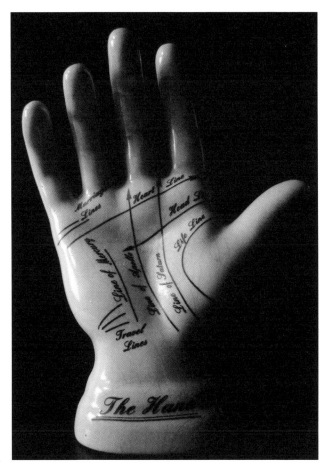

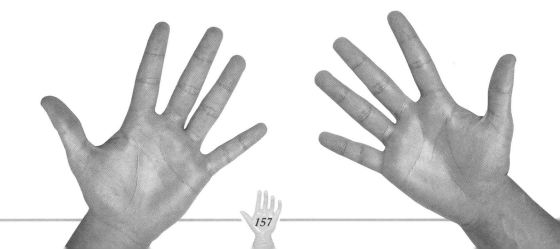

Index

A

angles 66
Apollo finger 32–33, 38
Apollo line 109–12
    end 111–12
    events 111
    start 110
Apollo mount 57
astrology in palmistry 25, 27
attachment lines 116–22
    love and relationships 116,
       119–22
    number of lines 117–18

C

Cheiro 8
child lines 126–28
    disturbances 128
colour 145
cross marks 134
curve of intuition 131

E

early palmistry 7–8
elements in palmistry, the 25

F

fate line 99–108
    direction 102
    end 108
    events 104
    lines joining 102–3
    moving 104–7
    start 101
    timing 102
fingernails 43
fingerprints 44–46
    arch 44
    composite 46
    loop 45
    peacock's eye 46
    whorl 45
fingers 20, 30–48
    Apollo 32–33, 38
    curled 34
    inclination 32
    Jupiter 32, 35–36
    key to the 35–40
    Mercury 34, 39–40
    phalanges 47–48
    relaxed 34
    Saturn 32–33, 36–37
    setting 31
fingertips 41–42
    thick or thin 43

G

general appearance 145

H

handprints, taking 152–55
hands 7, 12–19, 23
    backs of 29
    colour 22
    map of 26
head line 79–86
    straight, sloping
      or curved 82–84
    variations 85–86
healing striate 115
health 142–51
    colour 145
    general appearance 145
    indicators 148–51
    major lines 147–48
    rascettes 146
    temperature 145
health line 113–15
heart line 87–96
    disturbed lines 92–93
    friendships 94
    health on the heart line 96
    mystic cross 95
    variations 96
    where to start 88–91

J

Jupiter finger 32, 35–36
Jupiter mount 55

L

life line 70–78
    end of the line 77–78
    extra lines 77
    forked 73
    starting point 72
lines 67–130
    Apollo 109–12
    attachment 116–22
    child 126–28
    curve of intuition 131
    fate 99–108
    head 79–86
    health 113–15
    heart 87–96
    life 70–78
    minor 130–31
    rings and girdles 129–30
    sibling 128
    simian and semi-simian
      97–98
    temporary 48
    travel 123–25
lower Mars 26
Luna mount 60–61, 62

M

marks 132–35
    cross, the 134
    square, the 133
Mars
    lower 26
    plain of 26
    upper 26
Mars mount 63–64
Mercury finger 34, 39–40
Mercury mount 58
minor hand 14
mounts 54–65
mystic cross, the 95

N

Neptune mount 65

P

palmistry 8
    psychic 9
    scientific 9
phalanges 47–48, 51–53
plain of Mars 26
Pluto mount 62
psychic development 156–57
Pythagoras 7

R

rings and girdles 129–30

S

Saturn finger 32–33, 36–37
Saturn mount 56
sibling lines 128
simian and semi-simian lines
    97–98
skin-ridge patterns 136–41
square marks 133

T

thumbs 20, 48–53
    phalanges 51–53
    setting and inclination 49
travel lines 123–25
    disturbances 125

V

Venus mount 58–60, 62

Acknowledgements

All illustrations by Peter Mallison.
Photography by Colin Bowling.
Image page 8 © Getty Images.

Bibliography

The Living Hand (The Aquarian
Press, 1986).
Palmistry (Carlton, 1996).
Learning Palmistry (Caxton, 2000).